W9-CIJ-164

Praise for *Just Ask Leadership*

"While I honestly wasn't conscious of it, Gary's notion of 'leading by asking' nicely captures my own style. This approach creates a more collegial attitude. It opens dialogue and shows respect for those who are closer to and have responsibility for the issues. In many cases, it is also appropriate because each generation seems to be smarter than the last. As a tool, Gary's book can raise everyone's awareness of the social and intellectual power of asking rather than telling."

—**Tom Pritzker,** chairman, Hyatt Corporation and Marmon Group Holdings

"Gary will help leaders on the front line be much more effective. Asking questions is not just about decision making, it is what leaders use to lead!"

—**General Jack Chain**

"For innovative thinking and getting a new slant on an old problem, Gary Cohen is incomparable. He brings his rich background in growing a business and transforming it and himself to everything he does."

—**Marcy Syms,** CEO, Syms Corporation

"Gary Cohen's Just Ask approach to leadership made me question my own habit of 'leading by example.' Is it not more proactive to lead by provoking a response instead of requesting a spectator? And, is it not ultimately more productive by reacting to new solutions instead of judging redundancies?"

—**Vance Van Petten,** executive director, Producers Guild of America

"Gary's concept of Just Ask leadership is new and illuminating. It is what we do as leaders. Gary has brought unconscious competence in the world of leadership into our consciousness."

—**Matt Wisk,** president of MyPoints.com and executive vice president/chief marketing officer of United Online (NetZero)

"I think Gary's Just Ask leadership approach is an insightful and unique way of looking at the leadership problem that will give leaders a very definite way of putting positive leadership into practice. In other words, taking your ego out of it, listening to your people—those positive leadership attributes that I think are important."

—**Rear Admiral James A. Symonds,** Commander of Navy Region Northwest

"Good questions and active listening are the hallmark of great leaders in the private, public, and non-profit sectors. Gary Cohen illuminates this pathway to excellence in his new book, with real insight to what makes a question 'good' and what to listen 'for.'"

—**John C. Read,** president and chief executive, Outward Bound

"Peter Drucker once said, 'There is nothing so useless as doing efficiently that which should not be done at all.' Gary Cohen, with his theory that leaders should ask questions and not dictate, is onto something big. Leaders today need to listen to and empower staff to sift through the maze of complex yet insignificant 'noise' in the business world. Listening carefully to those that touch the client is key to growing a sustainable business."

—**Alan J. Krause,** president and CEO, MWH Natural Resources, Industry & Infrastructure, Inc.

"Gary's Just Ask leadership methods work and are relatively simple to implement in any organization. He teaches you how to ask the right kind of question, not the 'let me grill you'–type question that creates barriers and ill will. If you aren't asking questions, it means you are not naturally curious—a clear sign of someone mired in the past."

—**GL Hoffman,** president and CEO, JobDig

"I discovered long ago that it is more important to ask the right questions rather than pretend that you have the right answers. Gary's approach would result in greater employee engagement leading to better results."

—**Harsh Pati Singhania**, managing director, JK Paper Limited

"What is your source of innovative ideas? Whom and how do you ask to get the really new and insightful stuff? Gary gets it! You ask those that interface with customers or those that make stuff all day, every day. And, he has researched the most effective questions to ask."

—**Bill McLaughlin**, chairman and CEO, Select Comfort

"This is my favorite kind of book! A fascinating way to learn how alteration in your approach to leadership can have radical effects on results. *Just Ask Leadership*, is a thoroughly engaging, well-researched book that has changed the way I run my business."

—**Kayle Neeley**, CEO, EZ Payroll & Staffing, and former vice president, Norwegian Cruise Line

"Gary Cohen's idea of 'question-based leadership' gets at the heart of what real leadership is all about—dropping the ego and using the power of questioning to stimulate others to think for themselves."

—**Audie Dunham**, chief operating officer, The Arthur Group

"Gary has hit the nail on the head. For most companies, their greatest resource is their people. If leaders don't ask what they know, a valuable corporate resource will have been wasted."

—**Steven Segal**, founding partner, J.W. Childs Associates

"Gary's Just Ask techniques empower employees to manage their own destiny, which empowers managers to become leaders. Managing my staff used to be like herding cats, but thanks to Gary's Just Ask methodology, I now find myself at the head of a pack of tigers."

—**Ken Clark**, founder/CEO, 1–800-Translate

"I have found Gary's Just Ask approach to be a very effective way to help others assume responsibility and free myself to focus on the areas that truly require my attention. This approach has helped elevate thinking throughout our organization, including my own."

—**Matt Van Slooten**, president, Carlson Real Estate Company

"Gary's unique style of probing the most basic human behaviors sets him apart from many management gurus. He forces introspection, gets results, and motivates as few can. If you're really ready to examine your leadership style, this book is for you!"

—**Gary F. Beck**, vice president, Direct and Database Marketing Centex Homes

"Just Ask, applies to schools as well as businesses. Administrators can empower teachers and teachers can empower students simply by asking thoughtful, open-ended questions."

—**Arne Duncan**, United States Secretary of Education

"*Just Ask Leadership,* is today's version of Napoleon Hill's *Think and Grow Rich.*"

—**Marshall Besikof, CPA,** JD, LLM Partner, Lurie, Besikof, Lapidus & Company, LLP

"*Just Ask Leadership*'s strengths lie in its straightforward, unpretentious usefulness. It's a solid manual in a field that attracts a lot of gimmicky pretenders. . . . The questions are sound, and the approach is reassuring in its avoidance of any high-flown oversell. My first impression is of good principles usefully illustrated by someone who knows what he's talking about."

—**Ben Dunlap**, president, Wofford College (Spartanburg, SC)

"*Just Ask Leadership* integrates a number of key elements which are often not integrated in books of this nature (i.e. values, vision, asking the right questions). I found the examples from high-profile leaders to be more illuminating than inspiring, and I was happy with this."

—**Ted Love**, CEO, Nuvelo, Inc.

"I really like the specific examples that can be easily translated to business, volunteer and social/family situations. I like the short sections—excellent for a quick airplane or evening read without feeling like you have to complete the entire book or start over once you pick it up again. I also like how Just Ask can be applied to a broad cross-section in the organization—middle-management to leadership."

—**Cindy Chandler**, CEO, Chandler Group

"This is a leadership style with tremendous potential. The Just Ask method can have a profound effect on improving morale and make an organization more responsive as a whole. I also believe it would have a positive effect on staffing and training."

—**Michael Chwastiak**, founder, Blue Boulder

"Gary's vision is clear, simple, and compelling. The notion of asking as an alternative, or perhaps evolution from answering questions resonates and I think emphasizes something new in the business psyche."

—**David Cronin**, VP, American Express

"Leaders are often too tolerant of their own failures, and intolerant of others'. *Just Ask Leadership* helps leaders know when and how much to trust their coworkers. Cohen understands that to learn and grow, we all must have the opportunity to fail. He takes a long-term view of leadership that's refreshing and, in light of recent leadership failures at some of the nation's biggest companies, much needed."

—**Tom Oreck**, chairman, Oreck Corporation

JUST ASK
LEADERSHIP

WHY GREAT MANAGERS ALWAYS
ASK THE RIGHT QUESTIONS

GARY B. COHEN

New York   Chicago   San Francisco   Lisbon   London
Madrid   Mexico City   Milan   New Delhi   San Juan
Seoul   Singapore   Sydney   Toronto

The *McGraw·Hill* Companies

1 2 3 4 5 6 7 8 9 0 DOC/DOC 0 1 0 9

ISBN 978–0–07–162177–9
MHID 0–07–162177–6

McGraw-Hill books are available at special quantity discounts to use as premiums and sales promotions, or for use in corporate training programs. To contact a representative please e-mail us at bulksales@mcgraw-hill.com.

This book is printed on acid-free paper.

CONTENTS

FOREWORD

All good families have their epic stories, and the one my mother tells to every new guest in her Oregon home is "Young Harry's First Day of School."

When I slogged into our cramped kitchen after that first fall day in Mrs. Michaels' almost-as-cramped classroom, my mother naturally asked, "So what did you learn today, Harry?" I startled her with my reply.

"Nothing, mom," I said. "The teacher talked all the time."

Fortunately, part of what I learned, in school and away from it, is we overrate talking and misunderstand listening. You see that made vivid in those *Fortune* magazine corporate advertisements for companies who decide they must convince the world that they are "solution providers" by stressing their new theme, "We listen."

My work has convinced me that the creators of these ads misunderstand listening. Yes, listening helps you understand what others need. But the great successes come not from giving people what they want but from providing them with something they never could have imagined—iTunes, traveler's checks, and instant cash machines being three vivid examples.

No, people—clients and employees—value listening not because you will absorb what they hear and answer their need. They value listening for the act alone: being listened to makes them feel valued, and we treasure that feeling, as suggested by Richard Most: "The greatest gift you can give is the purity of your attention."

That helps explains why the man behind this book is well liked. When people talk, Gary listens. And because of how he listens—with all of himself, nonjudgmentally, gently—he encourages you to say what you couldn't, or hadn't, or wouldn't. And that points you in directions you never would have headed without him. Gary helps you see what you missed and achieve what you would have missed.

Although this appears to be a business book, it will enrich all of your life. Become a better manager and you will become a better parent, husband, and steward of your community, because those you manage are just like those whom you raise and live with: they are people, and what people love does not change when they cross the threshold into an office.

In business, Gary's approach has so many benefits that it's startling it's not used universally. Workers who, coaxed toward a solution of their own making, for example, feel a sense of authorship. They take responsibility and follow through; they work better and later. And at the end, they feel a pride of accomplishment that makes them more productive and motivated the next time, and on and on in the most virtuous of cycles.

Which brings me to Calvin Coolidge.

Before a dinner party that Coolidge was to attend, a woman bet her best friend that the president would say at least three words that evening. As the cake was being served, Coolidge had yet to speak. Fearful of losing her bet, the woman left her chair and approached his, bent over, cupped her hand, and whispered to him, "I bet Abigail that you would say at least three words tonight, Mr. President. What do you say?"

He replied, "You lose."

Yet this man who spoke so infrequently considered these words so vital that he left them to posterity: *No one ever listened himself out of a job.* He knew that people love listeners, value listeners, learn from listeners—and that they learn even more from us. But how can you listen even better, and reap all these rewards? You can start right now: stop listening to me, and start listening to this wonderful little book.

—Harry Beckwith

To Chris, Sammi, and Ali

ACKNOWLEDGMENTS

I am not the likeliest candidate to write a book. Severe learning challenges have always made writing difficult for me. I became so frustrated and dispirited in grade school that my mother hired a tutor, Pat Zimmerman, to assist me. I owe a debt of gratitude to my mother and Pat, as well as two helpful teachers, Craig Falkman and Sue Merriman. They encouraged me to push my way through challenges, put my thoughts down on paper, and lean on others to maximize my talents.

I am all for challenges, but a book seemed too big a project for me to "push through." At his cabin one afternoon, Bill McLaughlin (CEO of Select Comfort) convinced me otherwise. He said that I needed to write this myself. He couldn't have been more right and, in a way, completely wrong.

The words here are largely my own, but it has become a much bigger collaboration than I ever anticipated. I am especially indebted to all the leaders who shared their stories with me. I accumulated hundreds of hours of interviews on tape. Each of these leaders' stories became another stitch in the mosaic of this book (even if not all are overtly mentioned), and these leaders convinced me of the vitality and validity of question-based leadership.

This book never would have come together, though, if I didn't have an amazing family to lean on. Chris and the girls, Ali and Sammi, kept me rooted. Chris gave me the space and time to work, and was my inspiration throughout. The three of them had to put up with a sluggish husband, dad, and friend through some long stretches, and they helped me find ways to recharge. Together, we push and support each other, always.

My friends who helped are numerous, and some deserve special mention: my business partner of 18 years and close friend, Rick Diamond; our wonderful COO Dana Olson; and Senior Vice President Lois Dirksen, who was my left and right arm at ACI and remains a dear friend. Together, we learned and shared so much—from each other, our mentors, and through trial and error (sorry about some of those trials and errors, by the way!).

Thanks also to my friends Kayle Neeley, Marcy Syms, David Rochlin, and Phil Levin, who helped me sort through the ideas and concepts that appear in these pages. I deeply value our ongoing conversations and friendship. I feel similarly about Scott Richards, who sadly passed away last year, but whose presence is still felt.

I owe a huge debt of gratitude to my clients, who have trusted me in helping them and their organizations grow, and for their contributions to the Just Ask leadership model.

Harry Beckwith deserves a huge thank you as well, for his willingness to write the foreword and his insightful comments on drafts of the book. He is one of the world's best copywriters, and I am fortunate to count him as a friend. I will forever remember his advice: "The true cost to readers is not the price of the book, but the price of their time." I have tried to honor that advice on every page of this book.

I am perhaps most grateful to Harry for introducing me to Eric Vrooman, who worked with Harry on his first book, *Selling the Invisible*. Eric helped me organize and edit all the written material I generated for this book. He not only preserved my voice throughout, but also helped clarify my thoughts. I was proud, but not surprised, when the senior editors at McGraw-Hill expressed their amazement at how clean our draft was when it arrived!

I also had the privilege of working with David Brake, the CEO of the Content Connections. He and his staff (Holly McAllister, in particular) provided us with focus groups and sophisticated response technology, so that we could ask readers what they wanted and how we did at delivering against those wants. *Just Ask* received better grades and reviews than all but one of the bestsellers that we were matched up against, but thanks to David and his staff (and all the wonderful input from readers), the book is now vastly improved.

David worked with John Larson at Bright House Agency to get my book in front of the largest and best publishers in the world. The deal would not have happened without either of them.

I want to thank Mary Glenn for her fierce determination to make this a great book and for putting up with all of my questions! Even though it wasn't the top pick for her or her team (or for me, for that matter), Mary agreed to name the book *Just Ask Leadership* because that was the consensus pick of hundreds of early readers. Thank you, Mary and readers, for believing in and helping to shape this project.

I have learned so much from the brilliant leaders I interviewed. Many of them have since spoken to me about how awareness of their own questioning style has helped improve them as leaders. With their encouragement, I forged a partnership with Brian Ferro and Keith Morical to develop the Just Ask Leadership training course and a unique Leadership 360 assessment tool (which can be found at www.justaskleadership.com). I would be remiss if I didn't thank Brian and Keith for their terrific and visionary contributions as well.

The spirit of asking, and the process, have opened me up to so many new people and ideas, and I am extremely grateful for that.

INTRODUCTION

Would you rather be asked for your input or told what to do?

Good questions generate thought, focus, and action from the listener. They also convey respect. Maybe that's why 95 percent of leaders prefer to be asked questions rather than told what to do. And yet, according to a survey I conducted, these same leaders give instructions 58 percent of the time rather than asking coworkers for their input!

It's time for leaders to practice the type of leadership they most prefer themselves. If you want to lead and motivate others, questions are the answer.

I don't envision John F. Kennedy jumping onto his desk and telling everyone what to do during the Bay of Pigs. I imagine him asking his well-informed cabinet, "What do you think should be done?"

Leaders can't know everything—they couldn't in the 1960s, and they can't today. Especially not today. Information accumulates at such a rapid pace, and there are so many ways to access information, that our coworkers routinely know more about their work than we do.

If we tell our coworkers how to do their jobs, we are essentially limiting their options and stifling their initiative. We're not leading.

I grew up in a family of question askers. My grandfather cofounded Ellen Kaye Laboratories, the company that developed and produced Final Net Hair Spray (the first hair fixative to use a pump, not an aerosol bottle, thereby reducing ozone depletion). He often said, "Ideas are twenty-five cents a dozen. It's the person that runs all the way with one that succeeds." He valued workers who put ideas through a tough questioning process, as he did. His favorite question: "How will we hold off the bank a little longer?"

My mother was a psychotherapist and, prior to that, owned a chain of women's wear stores. Whether she was negotiating a conflict between sales personnel or listening to a client describe compulsive eating episodes, she found that one question brought clarity: "What is the purpose of their behavior?" Today, as an artist, she asks, "What do I wish to convey?"

My father was a top sales executive, representing John Meyer's upscale women's wear for 17 years. He asked department store buyers, "What other clothing lines are you showing?" to assess how much their customers were willing to spend. Once he had a sense of the buyer's vision, he presented options that filled several gaps. He customized his pitch based upon the buyer's needs, not his own preferences.

Questions served a different purpose for me. I suffered from a learning disability diagnosed in third grade, creating a wall that kept me from accessing knowledge in the same way other kids could. Asking questions became my way of getting around not knowing the answers. Despite my struggles, classmates came to me to discuss their problems and share successes. When this pattern continued through college, I grew more conscious of the connection between asking questions and leading others.

Thoughtful and open-ended questions often trigger unexpected connections. As an intern for Jim Ramstad, a Minnesota state senator, I had difficulties responding to constituents' mail due to my learning challenge. When I asked Jim, "What kind of meaningful legislation could I work on instead?" he suggested drunk-driving reform. Rather than type letters, I made inquiry calls. I asked invested organizations, "If you could create a law regarding drunk driving, what would it be?" The result was a bill that representatives from MADD (Mothers Against Drunk Drivers), local detoxification centers, and the sheriff's department all supported—one that made both Jim and me proud.

After college, my childhood friend Rick Diamond and I pooled $4,000 and began a two-person business in telecommunications. In a relatively short amount of time, we had over 2,200 employees and more than 20 Fortune 500 clients. Question asking was the pillar of our success. Rick and I could never know or do everything. We depended on the knowledge and expertise of those we led. When we didn't know, which was often, we asked.

I fought my ego constantly. If you're like me, your ego propelled you into leadership. You used your creativity and resourcefulness to meet objectives—a reduction of resources, for example, or an increase in revenue. You asked questions only to accomplish a specific task. In general, however, your ego discouraged you from asking questions and disliked following orders. Egos want to achieve—on their own.

Egos also crave recognition. With each success, your career has progressed and your standing in the organization or community has grown. Your ego has grown, too. You tend to ask fewer questions and provide more answers. After all, others—even your boss, perhaps—come to you as an oracle. You likely feel, and are, in control.

Here's the paradox: egos can vault you into a leadership position, but as a leader you now must set your ego aside and relinquish control.

As a leader, your career advancement is no longer task-dependent. Leadership is about allowing others the chance to flourish. You advance as a leader only when you place your coworkers' egos above your own. And you do that, and convey that, by asking questions.

Four-star general Jack Chain is a true leader. When he served as a staff officer in the Pentagon, his 10-year-old daughter asked him, "What do you do?" He thought for a minute and said, "I answer questions." Later, when he made commander, his daughter asked how his new role would be different.

His response: "Now I ask the questions."

Now you should, too. That's the message of this book: "Just ask." Here you will learn not only specific questions to ask in certain contexts but also how to implement question-based leadership as a whole. Rest assured, I won't ask you to play a character named "Leader" or require you to memorize lists. You will certainly *not* be expected to imitate Jack Welch or Gandhi. I want to help you lead authentically, and I have taken great care in making this book work for *you* rather than you for *it*.

By asking questions and empowering your coworkers, you will reap the benefits of their productivity and creativity. When everybody has a hand in an organization's decisions and future, their work is produced with the richness of a live performance. They improvise solutions when mistakes happen and respond to feedback. In addition, the more decision makers you have, the more likely faulty assumptions will be uncovered and amended.

The right question can empower, inspire, and challenge—both you and your coworkers. After all, open-ended questions engage the responder and the asker. They enable both to work together toward an uncertain and exciting end.

The chapter entries are short and center around real stories from some of this country's best leaders. When I set out to write this book, I didn't presume to have all the answers, so I asked. I interviewed almost one hundred highly effective leaders—religious leaders, Fortune 500 CEOs, small business owners, military commanders, heads of nonprofits, and so on. I asked them how they used questions to inform their strategic decisions. I asked them to describe various business and management scenarios and walk me through the kinds of questioning strategies that they felt were both effective and ineffective. I asked them how questions could make their organizations more competitive, more profitable, and better places to work.

These leaders don't equate asking questions with not knowing the answers. They don't believe that the only purpose in asking a question is to find an answer. They know that questions lead to fresh ideas, committed action, and the creation of a new rank of leaders.

You will get the benefit of their expertise throughout this book. You will also benefit from the input of early readers. Before submitting the manuscript to publishers, I invited readers to provide feedback in the form of surveys and focus groups. Based on this feedback, I cut an entire chapter, reorganized the table of contents, changed the title, and wrote entries to fulfill specific requests for content.

While most of the stories here come from the business community, you don't have to be a CEO to be a leader. Parents can be terrific leaders. So can soccer coaches. So can volunteers or temporary workers. Question-based leadership is valuable and appreciated in all spheres. The more you practice it, the more applications you'll find.

I promise that by the time you reach the end of the book, you will be asking more and better questions. Most importantly, your need to *tell* will decline as you increasingly recognize the limitless power of *asking*.

The leader of the past was a person who knew how to tell. The leader of the future will be a person who knows how to ask.

—PETER DRUCKER

CHAPTER 1

IMPROVE VISION—GAINING INSIGHT FROM ALL LEVELS OF THE ORGANIZATION

Questions can help us to see ourselves, coworkers, and organizations more clearly. In this chapter, you will learn to put your values and goals to the test with questions. Be sure to align these individual values and goals with the organization's on a regular basis. Your organization's culture and stability can be compromised, especially when new people are being hired, if you and other leaders don't communicate a unified vision. But once that vision has been established, focus on achieving long-term goals and spend less time managing short-term crises.

1. What are my values?
2. Are my values in alignment with the four core human drives?
3. Are our values as strong as our profits?

4. Is there a gap between our stated values and our operating values?

5. What is our organization's culture?

6. Are my coworkers aware of the importance of their work?

7. How true are the stories we tell?

8. Are job performance measures aligned with our organization's goals?

9. How can we outrun the competition?

10. Why is it my job to explore the unexplored?

11. How would I feel if this issue made the front page of the newspaper?

12. Am I a decision maker or goal achiever?

13. Am I leading into the future or am I managing the present?

14. What is my guiding question?

15. Is our organization asking the right question?

16. Who will be my successor?

17. How do I hire someone who will excel in our organization's culture?

18. If we hire this person, what should we expect?

Improve Vision #1:

What are my values?

Values drive our behavior, and yet most people don't catalog and rank their values—at least not explicitly. So when their values come into conflict with one another, they make rash decisions, allow themselves to be influenced by others, or fail to act.

Isolate and weigh your values now, when you're not under duress. (Note: You can do so for free at www.ceotest .com). In the future, you'll be more prepared to make quick, confident decisions and defend your position. More importantly, you'll know what your position is.

Suppose you learn that one of your coworkers lied on her résumé. In fact, she lied not only about her job title but also about her salary and the length of time she worked at a particular job. You learn about this lie when talking to her former employer at a trade show. The discovery takes you completely by surprise. After all, this person has worked for you for three years and done an outstanding job as vice president of sales, outperforming her two predecessors. To the best of your knowledge, she's been honest with you during her tenure, and you've grown to think of her as a friend. So, what should you do about the falsified résumé?

Without knowing your core values, you will be forced to make a decision while being clouded by emotional bias. You might be so emotionally enmeshed that you fail to make a decision and just let the matter slide. After all, any number of values might be coming into conflict: fellowship, loyalty, forgiveness, wealth creation, honesty, integrity, consistency, and so on.

If you previously ranked your values, you'll be prepared to handle this complicated scenario. If fellowship, loyalty, forgiveness, and wealth creation are of greater value to you than honesty, integrity, or consistency, then

11

your decision is clear. You'll keep her. If not, you must let this coworker go. If you've been clear about your values all along, this coworker and friend will respect your decision, and you'll sleep easier.

Once you've done the hard work of ranking your values, you'll see life through a new lens. Your relationships will improve. Your family, friends, and coworkers will sense and benefit from the clarity you will then have. They will come to know you better as a person and trust you to make decisions that are consistent with the values you espouse. And you will see them differently, too. You will have a better understanding of how your values overlap with theirs and where they diverge.

Improve Vision #2:

Are my values in alignment with the four core human drives?

In *Driven: How Human Nature Shapes Our Choices* (Jossey-Bass, 2002), two eminent Harvard professors, Paul R. Lawrence and Nitin Nohria, identify four core human drives:

- The drive to *acquire* stems from the basic human instinct to survive. It can be seen in our efforts to gather food, status, and power.
- The drive to *bond* is based on our need to connect with others for reproduction, social interaction, sharing/trading, and protection from predators.

- The drive to *learn* allows us to accumulate and transmit knowledge from generation to generation. This is where we develop our beliefs about how the world works or ought to work—ideologies, in other words (something that distinguishes humans from animals).
- The fourth drive, to *defend*, protects us from environmental risks by encouraging us toward fight or flight. In many ways, it takes into account all the other drives since we are called to defend not only our bodies but also our possessions, power, relationships, knowledge, and ideologies.

While these four drives often work synergistically, one or more can dominate. And, as with values, our drives can come into conflict. If there is limited food after a shipwreck, for instance, would your drive to bond with survivors impel you to share the food, or would your drive to acquire and survive supersede it?

Naturally, our drives are connected to our values. We settle on our values, in large part, based upon our needs to acquire, bond, learn, and defend. Examine your core values. Are all four drives represented in your choices? If not, reflect on the drive(s) not being satisfied and consider whether or not it points toward an unbalanced approach to your life. To be balanced doesn't mean that each drive has an equal and corresponding number of values. These drives have an innate desire to be met, however. If you're ignoring one, the situation bears some investigation and, perhaps, a realignment of your values.

Think of your prioritized values as a constitution. Try your best to live up to the spirit of them, but don't get caught up in constantly defending your position to yourself or others. Constitutions are, by their nature, somewhat elastic. Give yourself permission to be kind so that you and others aren't overwhelmed with shame and anger when acting in opposition to your values.

For example, if someone calls you a liar—and honesty, integrity, authenticity or trust are some of your core values—your first reaction will likely come from your drive to defend. After all, if you don't defend your core value, your self-image will suffer. Before you fly into full battle mode, ask yourself, "Have I ever lied?" If the answer is yes, then you are, in fact, a liar. Accept that you and others do lie on occasion but that you do your best to live up to the spirit of your values. Rather than counterattack your accuser, take it as an opportunity to illustrate how you employ your values in your daily life and explain how exceptions to your behavior don't rest easy with you.

Improve Vision #3:
Are our values as strong as our profits?

Are you willing to lose money or let your organization fail in order to maintain your values?

Marketing Architects purchases blocks of radio time and fills them with direct-response advertising. This

Minneapolis company's goal is to have its annual revenue become its net profits four years later. The company also believes in standing by its values, one of which is "the consistent development of strong, structured and knowledge-based relationships in every aspect."

When the terrorist attacks of September 11, 2001—9/11—hit, the entire advertising community trembled. Many companies reneged on their advertising commitments or pulled a high percentage of their ads off the air. Chuck Hengel, chairman and CEO of Marketing Architects, asked his team, "Should we cut back on our purchases?"

The response back was unanimous: "No. Business as usual." Team members felt a moral imperative to stick by their commitments and clients, and their value of maintaining strong relationships. Marketing Architects not only honored its agreements to purchase air time from large national radio networks, the company offered to offset its clients' shortfalls because of lower-than-expected response rates! When the networks and Marketing Architects' clients heard this news, they couldn't contain their disbelief and gratitude; some of them literally cried on the other end of the line.

In the aftermath of 9/11 more people listened to radio than before, and the response rates went through the roof. Rather than covering shortfalls, Marketing Architects "printed money" for its clients. The firm stuck by its values and was handsomely rewarded. Of course, the outcome could have been different. The company's honor and integrity would likely have been rewarded down the line, though—even if their actions had resulted in considerable short-term losses.

Once the Federal Aviation Administration (FAA) lifted the air travel ban that went into effect immediately following the attacks from the air on 9/11, Marketing Architects sent its sales force out to increase market share. Proud of their value-driven decisions, salespeople didn't have trouble securing new accounts. No surprise: People want to do business with honorable partners.

Don't choose profits over values. Choose values and trust that profits will follow. Ask, "What's the right thing to do?" and let the answer determine your course of action.

Improve Vision #4:
Is there a gap between our stated values and our operating values?

"Organizations must distinguish between stated values, those that hang on the wall, and operating values, those that are acted upon every day," says John Foley, CEO and founder of LEVEL, a brand and reputation firm. He urges organizations to align these values because of the massive impact a discrepancy can have on their brand and because it's the right thing to do.

Not every organization has stated values, but they all have operating values. Decisions are made every day by your coworkers, based upon their own values and their perception of the organization's values. They are keenly aware of how hard others are working, for instance, and whether or not their coworkers are respectful of the organization's mission, customers, and workplace.

The more explicit the organization's values, the more likely people will share and organize around them. Have you ever noticed how some organizations keep workers longer and make them happier (even without advancement opportunities or substantial pay increases)? Chances are that it's because the operating values are in line with the organization's stated values.

If you're happy with the operating values of your organization, make them explicit. Make them the stated values, and watch your brand/organization coalesce around them. If you're not happy with your organization's operating values, it will take longer for a positive culture to take shape.

17

If you haven't done so already, ask everyone in the organization:

- Who are we?
- What values do we possess?
- How do we want to behave?

Most organizations only involve the senior team in answering such questions and then later ask why people are behaving counter to those values. Don't make this mistake. If you want your coworkers to stay longer than the national average (2.7 years), make them part of the process.

Once critical mass has been achieved, the company's values will soak into its very fabric and new hires will absorb them, too.

Improve Vision #5:
What is our organization's culture?

Humans live in the frozen tundra, deserts, massive cities, and tropical islands. As they adapt to their particular environments, they join together to secure their safety and prosperity. They form social contracts—agreements about the rights and duties of each individual.

Over time, as individuals, families, and tribes band together and the social contract strengthens, a *culture* emerges—a term that encompasses not only values but also shared beliefs, characteristics, and behavior.

Anthropologists often consider themselves "value neutral" as it relates to observing cultures. I can't make this claim. There are organizational cultures that work effectively and those that don't.

At United Parcel Service (UPS), drivers are taught how to stop, unbuckle, and start moving out of the truck all at the same time—a process that saves the company millions of dollars. By installing global positioning systems (GPS) in its trucks, the company has reduced idle time considerably, again resulting in huge savings. UPS trucks drove 2.5 billion miles in 2006, so reducing fuel consumption must be a centerpiece of the company's culture, and it is. This is an ever-improving culture at work.

According to John Lilly, a 20-year veteran at Procter & Gamble who had responsibilities for over 30 different consumer brands, questions were seen as an opportunity to "explore possibilities." "We would look at a product and ask question after question, 'What if . . . ?'" In that culture, pride didn't get in the way of greater exploration. He and his colleagues used questions to improve their own work habits and the company's products.

When he became CEO of Pillsbury, John found that the company had a considerably more competitive and less cooperative culture. Questions were used to catch someone off-guard or unprepared, and in doing so, enhance the status of the asker. Because of the pride they invested in their work, Pillsbury workers took offense at such questions. Of course, this led to more insular behavior and a spirit of distrust.

Cultures develop, intentionally or unintentionally, so don't leave this matter to chance. Ask yourself the following questions:

- What is our organization's culture?
- Is our culture in alignment with our industry?
- Is our culture in alignment with the organization's mission and vision?
- Is our culture open to questions?

In *Leadership on the Line: Staying Alive through the Dangers of Leading* (Harvard Business School Press, 2002), Ronald A. Heifetz and Martin Linsky discuss at length how hard it can be to effect cultural change. Organizations can slide into parental hierarchies, especially when rules aren't clearly defined. Workers come to "Mom" and "Dad" for permission to move forward. But when questions are moving upward in your organization, not downward, the culture is bound to suffer. Questions should provide authority and power, not stand for permission.

It takes time to change any culture, and rarely does positive change occur without the bell-ringing endorsement of the leader. But once instigated, a strong organizational culture can be a dynamic, mountain-moving force—communicating and perpetuating a set of shared values, beliefs, and behavior.

Improve Vision #6:

Are my coworkers aware of the importance of their work?

Your legacy shouldn't just be a bronze sculpture in the lobby. It should be present in the air, in the culture, long after you're gone.

If you want to be remembered positively, you must ensure that the organization's values and behavior align. When they don't, you need to ask:

- What is causing this gap?
- What is the conversation we're not having?
- What can we do to solve this problem?

According to Mike Harper, former CEO of ConAgra, cultural change won't happen by ordering people to comply with the organization's values. Everyone must buy into these values individually. And leaders can only accomplish this by conversing with coworkers on an individual level.

Mike takes preemptive measures to make sure that gaps between values and behavior don't occur. He recounted for me a conversation he had with quality control inspectors on a bacon packaging line. These inspectors made sure that every pack of bacon met weight, color, and thickness specifications. He asked, "What happens if you don't do your jobs well?" The inspectors played out scenarios—customers getting ill, potential lawsuits, bad word of mouth, fewer repeat buyers, grocery stores not carrying their product, and so on. When Mike asked, "You know you have the most important job in the plant, right?" these inspectors knew he meant it. If they let the quality slip, even a little, the future of the entire company was in jeopardy.

Are your coworkers aware of the importance of their work? Are you? The more you recognize the importance of others, the more your organization's values and behavior will align, and the greater the legacy you will leave.

Improve Vision #7:

How true are the stories we tell?

We all have a unique perspective based upon our personal history, beliefs, values, behaviors, culture, and language. Our perspective takes the form of stories, which we craft to explain our successes and failures. In little league, we often struck out because we didn't have batting gloves and our coach didn't throw us curveballs in practice. These sorts of stories are usually a combination of subjective truth and fantasy. The more we tell them to ourselves, though, the harder it is for us to distinguish truth from fantasy. They crystallize into memory.

All our bodies' cells, including brain cells, regenerate every seven years, but our memories outlast them. If our memories are so stubborn, is it any wonder that we are, too? We cling tightly to the stories we've gathered and formulated. In essence, they are us.

We defend our stories vigorously in part because, as a unique blend of emotion and logic, they are hard to explain. We also have an investment in keeping some of them buried. If they're unearthed, then we might have to admit failure and revisit decisions we've made based on faulty logic. Exposing these stories, however, allows us to grow and develop perspectives that are grounded more in truth than fantasy.

It takes a culture of trust to get members of your organization to reveal what they believe and why they believe it. We must feel safe if we are to reveal our emotionally charged stories. For this reason, any *gaining-perspective* question you ask you must be willing to answer as well.

Here are a few examples of *gaining-perspective* questions:

What responsibilities or daily tasks are you tied to,
and why?

*What thoughts are triggered when you hear the
word fear?*

*Why did you react so strongly to the speech our
CEO gave?*

What keeps you up at night?

*What is the story behind the value you hold most
dearly?*

The stories we tell to ourselves and others aren't
always accurate. Be prepared to question their underpinnings—memories that may, in fact, be decades old and
in desperate need of revisiting.

To ensure safety—your own and that of others—be
sure to qualify these gaining-perspective questions by
saying that you are seeking only professionally related
responses, not personal ones.

23

Improve Vision #8:

Are job performance measures aligned with our organization's goals?

I asked Robert Fry, former executive vice president of
L.L. Bean, "What is the single most powerful question
you've ever been asked in your career?" The answer
came to him immediately, but before he shared it, he provided the context.

His company measured everything, which is a fairly
standard practice for companies that have grown up in
the direct marketing industry (e.g., catalog, direct mail,

call center, Web). But when an outside consultant asked, "What are the top two or three key measurements to know that you're reaching your goals?" the executive committee fell silent. According to Bob, "As you looked around the table you could sense a fear of not knowing. Each of us had plenty of key performance indicators in our departments, but none that as a company we could all agree on were the most important. It was totally shocking how a company this well organized and planned could be stumped by such a straightforward question."

The meeting wasn't a total loss. With the consultant's assistance, the executive committee hammered out what the top three key indicators ought to be: sales per catalog, return on investment, and business expenses as a percent of net sales.

Just because you've got your goals and budget in place doesn't mean you're done with strategic planning. Make sure that everyone is managing toward the same organization-wide goals. Not only will it help managers prioritize job performance measures, it will also help unify the whole organization.

Improve Vision #9:

How can we outrun the competition?

My business partner, Rick Diamond, CEO of ACI, has a saying over his desk that he got from Ted Deikel, former CEO and chairman of Fingerhut Corporation. It says:

Every day in Africa a gazelle wakes up.
It knows it must run faster than the fastest lion or it
will be killed.
Every morning a lion wakes up.
It knows that it must outrun the slowest gazelle or it
will starve to death.
It doesn't matter whether you are a lion or a gazelle.
When the sun comes up, you better be running.

—ABE GUBEGNA, ETHIOPIA, CIRCA 1974

Rick and I had no prior experience in the call center industry, so when we woke up in the morning, we knew we had to do at least one thing better than our competition; otherwise, our company would starve. We asked ourselves, "How can we outrun the competition? How can we improve upon what they do?"

We first narrowed our focus. How could we reduce the amount of dead time our call center operators spent on the phone? This question prompted us to seek the technology called "predictive dialing," which was being used in the collections industry. Predictive dialing eventually became the call center industry standard, but not before little ACI grew from two employees to 2,200. This technology predicted when operators were going to complete a call and transferred another call to them the moment they hung up. If call center operators normally spent 22 minutes an hour talking to customers, now they would spend 45. Because payroll was our largest cost, we were able to both outproduce and undercut the competition. As lions new to the territory—lion cubs really—we caught our first gazelle.

If you're chasing the competition, be a lion. Ask yourself: "How can we outrun the competition? How can we improve upon what they do?" If you're trying to stay ahead of the competition, run like a gazelle. Ask yourself: "How can we avoid being caught? What will allow us to increase the distance between us and the competition?"

Improve Vision #10:

Why is it my job to explore the unexplored?

The leader's role is to ask questions that aren't being asked by others. Everyone else in the organization can be demoted, circumvented, or replaced. Unless there's a strong overseeing board, the leader is largely immune to these concerns. The leader's only judges are banks and customers.

Too many leaders bathe in the light of their past accomplishments—what they built, what they own, how far they've come—when they should be investigating barriers and bridges to the future.

Some of your coworkers may have blinders on, doing only the work that's placed in front of them. Don't judge them too harshly, since they are vital to everyday operations. As a leader, though, you must have more peripheral and long-range vision. Climb up to the crow's nest for an unobstructed view. Take a look down at your ship's deck. What might be impeding your progress? Now look out to sea. What opportunities do you see on the horizon? What threats?

Tom Pritzker, chairman of Hyatt Corporation and Marmon Group Holdings, read in the *New York Times* one morning that pending legislation would require tobacco products to be moved behind store counters. Since at that time he owned a tobacco company, Conwood, he was understandably concerned. Conwood's CEO assured him the legislation would have a negligible effect on the company's business, since all companies would be beholden to the same rule, but Tom could see storm clouds looming. He asked for a breakdown of the legislation's effects by region and product line.

Despite some grumbling, the Conwood senior team ran the numbers. They assumed that consumers were the ones lobbying for the bill. It turned out, however, that big tobacco companies intended to use the bill to strangle their competition and prevent new entrants into the market. The big players, with their well-established brands, could demand that retailers purchase their whole line of products or none at all. Since space behind counters was limited and smaller competitors couldn't guarantee sales of their products, the littler companies were the ones who stood to lose. Tom's team estimated that the legislation would cost Conwood anywhere from 50 to 100 percent of its earnings.

Management then launched a deeper investigation into the commercial practices of their largest competitor. The

27

results suggested a pattern of anti-competitive behavior: the most notable example being the wanton and large scale destruction of Conwood's display racks by their competitor's salespeople. As an attorney, Tom had the view that these practices were a violation of antitrust laws, but management was averse to litigation. Eventually, however, he won them over and Conwood launched one of the largest antitrust suits ever in U.S. courts. This resulted in a $1.05 billion verdict in his favor and more importantly, resulted in an injunction which allowed Conwood to enter the market with an innovative, price-oriented product, which later captured a 40 percent market share in its category.

Tom salvaged what could have been a total disaster by asking early on, "How exactly will this decision impact our business?" and, "Who stands to gain or lose?"

Climb to the top of the mast and scan the sea for opportunities and threats. Then ask forward-leaning questions that others may be reluctant to voice.

Improve Vision #11:

How would I feel if this issue made the front page of the newspaper?

Feel-good stories rarely make the headlines, and meeting your organization's sales targets won't sell papers. Reporters don't wear rose-colored glasses; they look for dirt—especially on the wealthy, famous, and powerful. So before you make a controversial decision or sign off on a discretionary expenditure, imagine what the headlines might be.

Whenever we had an issue in dispute, Tom Madison, retired CEO of US West Communications and a board member of my former organization, asked, "How would you feel if this issue made the front page of the newspaper?" If he failed to ask that question, John Kunz, former president of Dun & Bradstreet, often did. They were well aware of what negative press could do to our company and careers.

Once a writer or news source takes a stand against you, you have little chance of reversing the tide. Your every comment will feel as if it's taken out of context, and the press won't necessarily stretch to get the full story. I recall an instance when only former members of our organization were interviewed for an investigative report, not current ones. Needless to say, the results were not good—or fair.

The papers are filled with stories about leaders who receive golden parachutes and performance bonuses, which leave employees and stakeholders feeling bitter—especially when health-care benefits and pensions are being cut. As a leader, you're in the limelight. So whenever you make a decision that could affect your image or the organization's, ask, "How would I feel if this issue made it to the front page of the newspaper?"

Improve Vision #12:

Am I a decision maker or a goal achiever?

At an executive retreat I attended, an expert consultant asked the assembled leaders, "Why do you get paid?" After listening to a variety of responses, he revealed his answer: "Leaders get paid for making decisions." He's right, to a point, but the message he sent was a dangerous one for leaders to hear.

Yes, leaders make decisions, but if they think of themselves as decision makers, that's what they'll be. Not leaders. Decision makers organize their universe around problems. In general, they seek to define a problem, solicit input, create a desired outcome, and then select a strategy.

Exceptional leaders don't start with the problem. They start with the organization's *goal*. Next, they assess the current state of the organization in relation to the goal—the organization's *position*, in other words. The third step is to determine the *strategy* to reach the goal from the current position.

Although these two approaches are similar, they are not the same, and the difference in outcomes can be dramatic. The goal achiever works from a proactive state (where do we want to go?). The decision maker works from a reactive state (how are we going to get out of this situation?). Goal achievers lead and inspire their coworkers as they head toward a concrete destination. They want to do the right thing. Decision makers seek personal recognition, engender distrust, and go where the wind takes them.

Authority figures in hierarchical organizations who consider themselves decision makers do so because as they moved up through the ranks, they rode the coattails of their clever decisions. Exceptional leaders, who demonstrate leadership, inspire those beneath them to make sound decisions. If leaders are making all the decisions, there are fewer opportunities for their coworkers to excel. And these leaders are not spending enough time or effort identifying their organization's overarching goal, position, and strategy (what I call "GPSing"). This process works just like a GPS: you supply the destination (goal), the system triangulates your location (position) relative to the destination using a satellite, and then it produces accurate and efficient directions (strategy).

31

Start using GPSing, if you're not already. With questions, focus in on the goal, identify the organization's current position, and then search for the correct strategy. Think of yourself as a goal-achieving leader, not a decision maker.

Improve Vision #13:

Am I leading into the future or am I managing the present?

David McLaughlin, former chairman of the Red Cross and past president of Dartmouth College, said that he always knew whether he was leading or managing. If he was handling issues that were one to five years out, he was leading. If the problems were closer to the present, he was managing.

Leaders are responsible for vision—both their vision and the vision of their coworkers. Ideally, the distance workers see into the future increases as they move up in the organization:

- Front-line workers should consider their work from a minute, hour, day, and week perspective.
- Supervisors should consider their work from an hour, day, week, and month perspective.
- Managers should consider their work from a day, week, month, and quarter perspective.
- Vice presidents should consider their work from a week, month, quarter, and annual perspective.
- Presidents should consider their work from a month, quarter, annual, and three- to five-year perspective.

Each succeeding level in the organization ought to eliminate one line of microexamination and add an additional view of macroexamination. This doesn't mean that front-line workers aren't aware of the overall goals for the company or that presidents can't spend some time working on present-time issues; it simply means that everyone must be responsible and accountable for his or her own goals to achieve the goals of the organization.

Do you spend the bulk of your time forecasting into the future (*leading*, in other words) or *managing* short-term crises? If you're focused more on the present than on the future, pass those present-day responsibilities onto the managers and supervisors, where they truly belong. If you don't feel confident that your managers and supervisors can handle these responsibilities, you're either too controlling or you need to hire better people.

Improve Vision #14:

What is my guiding question?

"*Om . . .*" Meditators use sounds like this one to help them find peace, harmony, and direction. These sounds are repeated until the day's irritations—sirens, horns, slips, spills, criticisms, and so on—slip away.

33

Guiding questions can have a similar harmonic effect. They can make sorting through distractions and options much easier. Not surprisingly, many leaders find them invaluable. Greg Farrell, president and CEO of Expeditionary Learning Outward Bound, said to me, "You know, Gary, the question I'm wrestling with is not 'Should I work with a guiding question?' but 'What guiding question should we work with when setting up each expeditionary learning model?'"

Guiding questions serve to reinforce larger goals—your own or your organization's. My goal in writing this book was to share the value of question-based leadership with readers. To help me achieve that goal, I knew I needed a guiding question. After much thought, I settled on "Why is it that exceptional leaders spend so much time asking questions?"

The experience of writing a book, like building a business or organizing an event, is filled with many interesting distractions. Without my guiding question I might have been redirected by my research and curiosity, and wound up writing a book on sailing, or entrepreneurs, or a 40-volume encyclopedia. Instead, when I reached a crossroad, I simply asked, "Am I writing and researching the right material to answer my guiding question?" No matter how interesting or important the new information was, I made sure it helped answer my overarching question. If it didn't, I pushed it aside or filed it away for future projects.

When you're writing a book, the consequences of your decisions are largely yours alone to suffer. In an organization, many more lives are affected. Don't make your coworkers follow your every whim. What overarching question are you trying to answer? Once you have settled on a question, let it guide you. Repeat it daily like a meditation sound. And periodically ask, "Am I asking the right question?" Keep asking this question until your heart and mind come together.

Improve Vision #15:

Is our organization asking the right question?

While Sears focused on the question, "What do our customers want?" Wal-Mart asked, "Where do our customers want to shop?" Look where they are now. Sears is fighting for survival, and Wal-Mart is experiencing almost unfathomable growth and prosperity.

"I'm never afraid, especially given the characteristics of this organization, that we won't come up with a decent answer. I worry when we haven't asked the right question," said Bob Senkler, CEO and chairman of Securian Financial.

"How does this decision allow us to meet our promise to pay?" is the right question for Bob and Securian, since they're in the insurance business and aware of their customers' primary fear: failure to pay claims.

With "variable life" products, customers can get a higher possible return, but the exact amount can't be guaranteed. "This doesn't meet our organization's 'promise to pay,'" many of Bob's coworkers argued. Bob asked the team, "If we don't offer this product and it takes off in the marketplace, will we retain our sales force and organizational strength?" The answer was no. Bob then successfully argued that sustaining financial strength (through the inclusion of variable life products) was essential to maintaining their promise to pay.

Make sure your organization is asking the right question. And don't hesitate to revisit, or reinterpret, that question to address shifts in the marketplace.

Improve Vision #16:

Who will be my successor?

Harry Levinson, a former Harvard and MIT professor who has written extensively about the psychology of leadership, went to a celebration at Brandeis University, honoring their newly appointed president. Harry asked the new president, "Whom have you chosen as your successor?" Another member of the faculty became quite agitated by Harry's question, especially as it was the first day of the new president's reign. The president, however, wasn't rattled. He understood the wisdom of the question.

Several years earlier the president of Brandeis University and his wife were killed in a fire at their hotel in Egypt, and the university went through a difficult transition. In his work as a management consultant, Harry observed the consequences to many organizations when the leader abruptly left. With time to plan, organizations can develop leaders and ensure smooth transitions. Without that time, the search for leadership can be draining and extensive. The culture can become unstable, unmoored, and unprepared to accept someone from the outside.

Having a successor, even if it's just an interim position, can provide much needed stability.

Regardless of your position in the organization, you ought to know the answer to Harry's question. Whom have you pegged as your successor?

Improve Vision #17:

How do I hire someone who will excel in our organization's culture?

When hiring, employers often consider an individual's unique skill set, knowledge, and pedigree. What they sometimes don't consider are the ways this individual might change the organization's culture.

Every organization with two or more members is a *system*. Within a system, each individual is connected, directly or indirectly, with every other individual. As the number of members increase, the web of connections becomes more and more complex. Because of the systemic nature of organizations, any new individual necessarily impacts every other individual. Consequently, those charged with changing an organization's membership—by firing, hiring, or transferring—have a serious responsibility. Their decisions must be goal-oriented, purposeful, and wise.

As a coach, I find many leaders mistakenly focus on filling gaps with *skills and knowledge* rather than with *people*. "We need someone who can sell!" "We need a tax accountant!" "We need a Ph.D. for this research!" Posted positions describe necessary skills and degrees. And interview questions are aimed at discovering details about the skills and degrees listed on résumés.

"Larry" (an acquaintance of mine, who prefers to go unnamed) owns a sizeable consulting firm. He hired two new partners, each with exceptional investment banking skills. Larry was sure these two would become major revenue producers (or "rainmakers") for his company. What he didn't consider was their cultural "fit." His company and its success had been built on trust, honesty, and, above all, teamwork. The new hires had two different values: self-interest and personal gain. Within a year, they nearly destroyed the firm—not because they lacked skills or knowledge, but because they disrupted a once stable culture. It quickly changed from one of trust and concern to one of distrust, cynicism, and triangulating conversations. A year passed before Larry recognized the crashing waves and turned to action, firing the two employees. Once they were gone, the company—like most systems—returned to its optimal functioning state.

One of the most powerful tools a leader has is the ability to influence an organization's culture. When a leader fires an employee or hires a new one, a message is sent regarding both the leader's values and the organization's standards. In the case of Larry's consulting firm, employees did not speak up, mainly because they thought their leader had made a deliberate choice. They assumed he was trying to move the company in a new, more independent direction. It was only when tensions reached the boiling point that they began to voice their concerns.

Imagine that you're selecting a Supreme Court justice—one with the power to shift the Court's ideology and opinions for years to come. With so much at stake, don't you owe it to yourself and others to be certain of your choice?

Bring your coworkers in when conducting final interviews. Doing so helps ensure that the current culture will remain consistent and the organization will remain purpose-driven. By *asking* for input during the hiring process—rather than *telling* coworkers about their new colleague—leaders reflect their desire to lead, not command and control. And your coworkers will feel a stronger investment in the future of the organization.

Improve Vision #18:

If we hire this person, what should we expect?

"What we look for in other beings is the hoped for satisfaction of our own desires."

—Simone Weil

Before hiring someone, ask, "Am I hiring this person to satisfy my needs or the organization's?" Often hiring happens quickly because of the leader's stake in the matter. Until a gap is filled, the leader may have to cover part (if not all) of the prospective worker's responsibilities— "doing" work, not "leading" work.

Leaders may hesitate to fire ineffectual or untrustworthy coworkers out of fear of not being liked, or because of the work involved with hiring and covering gaps. The longer these employees are kept on, the better prospective employees look. The desire to fill the position quickly combined with the desire for a skilled, trustworthy employee can, however, result in leaders feeling "selector's remorse" six months later.

Most leaders ask questions about past work performance, do background and reference checks, and test prospective employees with decision-making scenarios. What they fail to do is identify difficult or unpleasant traits. Interviews tend to focus on positive traits, so this shouldn't come as a surprise. But everyone has traits that can irritate others. If you don't uncover these traits in an interview, be wary. Chances are they exist.

Once you and your colleagues settle on a qualified candidate, ask, "Can we live with this person's negative traits, day after day after day?"

Be prepared to remind yourself and others that you decided to hire this candidate despite these traits. Over time, irritating traits might cloud your judgment. You see only the last wave hitting the shore, not the oceanic depths present in all people. You may miss the truly valuable contributions this coworker makes—the positive qualities and skills that tempted you to hire her in the first place.

Improve Vision Summary

Vision starts with an awareness of values: yours and the organization's. If you're acting in concert with both sets of values, then you will know the right thing to do when interacting with customers, hiring new employees, and setting goals. With clearly defined goals and guiding questions, you will inspire others to follow. As your coworkers learn the importance of their work and input, the organization's stated values will eventually become the operating values, and the culture will thrive.

40

"The important thing is not to stop questioning.
Curiosity has its own reason for existing."

–Albert Einstein

CHAPTER 2

ENSURE ACCOUNTABILITY— INCREASING TEAM AND ORGANIZATION-WIDE PERFORMANCE

If you groom leaders at all levels of your organization, work will get done well and on time. Rather than micromanaging (which stifles others' growth and creativity), spend your time focusing on job descriptions, resource allocation, and performance reviews. Question your accountability procedures, not your coworkers' work ethics.

1. Who's to blame—the employee or the job description?
2. Are my team leaders leaving a trail of frustrated people behind?
3. How often should I schedule performance reviews?

4. How do I get coworkers to stop repeating the same mistakes?

5. How can I entice coworkers to modify their behavior? (KiSS: Keep doing, Stop doing, Start doing)

6. Why do my coworkers ask me questions that they should (and often do) know the answers to?

7. Why are my direct reports coming to me with problems that are not my responsibility?

8. Am I an interrogator or an interviewer?

9. What am I afraid of losing?

10. How do I give coworkers maximum latitude to make their own decisions?

11. How can I reduce a coworker's fear of failure?

12. When should I commit resources to new projects?

Ensure Accountability #1:

Who's to blame—the employee or the job description?

When an employee isn't performing well, leaders often ask:

- Why didn't you reach your sales targets?
- How come you didn't finish that report on time?
- What skills do you need to add or improve?

Frustration builds on the part of the employee and the leader. And two dueling narratives take shape—"He's unreliable, unqualified, and a perpetual disappointment" (leader); "No matter what I do, how hard I try, I can't seem to accomplish my work and satisfy my boss's expectations. Why is it so hard to please her? Why do I even bother trying?" (employee). Both mount evidence to support their positions.

Sometimes, though, the job description is to blame.

It's a mistake, for instance, for the head of sales to also be in charge of service. The skills required for these two positions are incompatible. I know from personal experience. In the early days at ACI, I made a sales call at Sears after attending a humbling service quality meeting with our operations unit. I believe strongly in transparency and honesty—then and now. So how was I supposed to persuade Sears, in that moment, to choose our company over our competitors? The answer: I couldn't. Half my brain was focusing on how we needed to improve.

In my coaching business, I repeatedly find this problem, particularly in small companies where employees are asked to wear lots of hats. After hearing a diatribe of disappointment from a leader about an employee, I'll ask to see the employee's job description. After reading it, I'll hand it back to the leader and ask, "Could you do this job effectively?" The answer is often, "No." In fact, the leader finds it hard to imagine anyone who could do so. We then switch gears and start designing a job description that gives the employee a real chance to succeed.

Before you let a narrative of failure and disappointment take shape, ask, "Who's to blame—the employee or the job description?"

Ensure Accountability #2:

Are my team leaders leaving a trail of frustrated people behind?

Captain James A. Symonds commands the USS *Ronald Reagan*, a ship with over three thousand personnel. "Harry Truman said it best," says Symonds, "'It is amazing what you can accomplish if you do not care who gets the credit.'"

And yet Symonds admits that it can be hard to detect those who don't heed Truman's advice. "A lot of folks with too big an ego make it too far in this business because they look a lot better from above than they do from below." They get promoted because they're effective and efficient but "leave a trail of frustrated people behind."

When superiors don't value their opinions and involve them in the decision-making process, people feel unfulfilled and unappreciated, often to the point of quitting. The Navy is no exception to this rule. Just because people are expected to follow orders in the military doesn't mean they have to like it.

Symonds told me that the Navy was considering using 360-degree evaluations: a process that would reveal self-promoters because it incorporates feedback from superiors, peers, *and subordinates*. With 360s,

Navy brass could ensure that team leaders were developing other leaders, assigning challenging work, asking open-ended questions, and creating a fulfilling work environment.

Does the team leader who reports to you, the one you likely consider the best of the batch, look as good from below as he does from above? Ask the ones who know best—those who are below.

Ensure Accountability #3:
How often should I schedule performance reviews?

Henry Chidgey, who once ran several railroad and diamond companies, advocates monthly performance reviews. These reviews need not and should not be complex; they work best when kept extremely simple. Maximum accountability is the main goal.

Here's how the process works: The day before the meeting, your coworker brings you a list of five or six key objectives, detailing her progress on each. During the review on the following day, you simply assess the data and discuss how performance compares with objectives. Depending on the employee, this can be a short 30-minute process or it can take as long as two hours.

When an employee comes into your office, she should always bring a pen and paper and be required to take detailed minutes of the meeting. Once the meeting is over, the employee should make a photocopy of the minutes for your file. The reason for doing so is twofold: first, the notes allow you to verify the individual's understanding of the review; second, the notes increase consistency from one review to the next.

There are three key questions to ask during the meeting:

I. How well did you meet the objectives we mutually agreed on?

II. Choose one of the following:

   a) If you're ahead, how did you get ahead?

   b) If you're behind, how did you get behind?

   c) If you're on target, is there anything I need to know?

     1) If yes, discuss further.

     2) If no, extol the virtues of coming in on target.

     3) If you're not meeting your objectives, what's the root cause?

The third question should trigger a discussion. In it, remain objective and listen, giving your coworker time to sort through her answer. If you can accept her explanation of the "root cause," you allow it to be the actual root cause. If you can't accept this explanation, you become her coach, helping her better understand the situation.

Don't provide solutions; the employee needs to do this. If you *tell* rather than *ask*, you will not have accountable employees. Be patient. Having employees solve their own problems is critical to building their accountability.

Once the employee develops a solution, coach her through the following steps:

1. Establish an action plan.
2. Establish a deadline for implementing the action plan.
3. Schedule another meeting immediately after the deadline.

With difficult employees, you may need to increase the pressure, particularly if they consistently fail to meet goals. Pressure can be increased simply by increasing the frequency of reviews. The process can occur every two weeks, every week, or even daily, if needed. It's unlikely that daily reviews will continue long term, as an employee at this stage is usually on the way out.

The key is to remain on board with the employee, instead of playing the heavy. Let the progress reports do the hard work. An added benefit of the reports is that no goal will be overlooked for long without action being taken.

You might wonder, "If I manage like this, how will I ever get my own work done?" Consider the alternative. If your coworkers aren't accountable, you'll be doing their work for the rest of your career. Practice the Just Ask management style consistently, however, and most of your coworkers will require very little of your time.

In fact, they will likely become apostles of accountability, replicating your style throughout the organization.

Ensure Accountability #4:

How do I get coworkers to stop repeating the same mistakes?

I can ask my daughters three times to pick their clothes up off the floor and not get results. Rather than ask a fourth time, I'll just do it myself. Over time, my frustration builds. The 100th time I ask them to pick up their clothes, I might pull my hair, turn purple, raise my voice, and shock my daughters with an uncharacteristic and unreasonable response. Everyone feels aggrieved.

There's a way to avoid this stress and aggravation. Instead of asking simple yes or no questions, provide choices with real consequences. I might, for instance, ask my daughters, "Would you prefer picking up your clothes each morning or a receiving a 50 percent reduction in your allowance?"

In your organization, if someone keeps repeating the same mistake, make the stakes clear. Then allow that person to make a choice. Ask, "Do you want to be part of the team and start coming prepared to meetings, or would you rather move on?"

Some might find this practice a bit heavy-handed, but accountability begins with choice.

Make the choices and consequences clear. Obviously, there's a limit to how many times you can suggest the option of quitting or being fired before it loses its effectiveness. The stakes don't always have to be this high. Ideally, the consequences to the coworker should not be greater than the consequences of the repeated mistake are to you.

Ensure Accountability #5:

How can I entice coworkers to modify their behavior? (KiSS: Keep doing, Stop doing, Start doing)

Most people who try to lose weight are back at their original weight within three years. Smokers, drinkers, and drug users relapse at tragic rates, even those who go through treatment programs. When behaviors become ingrained, they're hard, very hard, to change.

Leaders are often unrealistic about their expectations for change. By the time they ask for change, their coworker's behavior is already driving them crazy. That's why they want and expect the change to take place immediately. Announcing that they'll be watching closely doesn't help matters. That creates paranoia and the desire to hide—the same feelings that prompt an alcoholic to store liquor in a shoebox and sneak a drink when nobody's looking.

When they demand change from coworkers, some leaders conveniently forget how hard change has been for them and how much time the process can take.

The acronym KISS (Keep It Simple, Stupid) has taken root in our collective consciousness. KiSS is a variation that I find helpful, if less memorable (in part because it really should be KeSS). Here's how it works. During your coworker's next review, ask, "What is the one thing you would like to KEEP doing, STOP doing, and START doing?" If your coworker doesn't own the need for change, the change is virtually guaranteed not to happen. The KiSS process encourages ownership.

If the coworker doesn't mention the behavior you want to see modified, raise the issue and explain why you would like that behavior changed. It is a review, after all. Ask if he will agree to make the change. Chances are he will, especially if you're not asking for more than three changes at any given time.

Let's say your coworker has had a difficult time responding promptly to phone calls. On average, he doesn't return two of your calls a week. If this is happening with you, his direct report, it is likely happening with customers, suppliers, and other staff. At the next review, you ask the coworker to return all calls within three hours, and he agrees to make this change.

Your coworker begins in earnest and does a remarkable job until three weeks later when he forgets to return a call from you. Not returning calls is a sign of disrespect, but blasting your coworker ("I knew you couldn't change!") isn't helpful. In fact, he might return to his old behavior out of spite.

Instead, reinforce the positive: "You've made tremendous strides on returning calls, which made me wonder if something happened yesterday that made it hard for you to get back to me."

Positive events carry less emotional memory than negative ones. Every time we switch lines at the grocery store, it seems like our former line moves faster. According to psychological researchers, we don't all have bad grocery store luck. We just remember the times that something didn't work and hold those memories longer and with greater intensity.

Celebrate positive changes and ask about (don't harp on) the setbacks.

Ensure Accountability #6:

Why do my coworkers ask me questions that they should (and often do) know the answers to?

A client of mine answered this question with another: "Why can't you tickle yourself?" According to *Scientific American*, the cerebellum tracks and foresees your hand's movement before you even move. This forward prediction neutralizes the response of other parts of the brain involved in being tickled.

This same type of neutralizing happens when a coworker has a question. This person comes into your office or catches you in the hall. All you have to do is restate their question, and more often than not they come to their own solution.

What seems to be happening in these interchanges is the giving of permission. Your coworkers are looking for validation that they actually have the right to solve a particular issue.

How you respond is important. If you provide the answer, you enter into the cycle of building dependence. Resist this urge and simply volley the question back.

Refrain from giving permission to the answer once it's provided. This practice is only marginally better than providing answers yourself, in terms of building up your coworkers' sense of responsibility and confidence. If they are the decision makers, let them decide.

Your coworkers can't tickle themselves. Tickle them with questions.

Ensure Accountability #7:

Why are my direct reports coming to me with problems that are not my responsibility?

If problems or "exceptions" keep landing on your desk—problems that truly are not your responsibility— you and your coworkers might have vastly differing opinions about your respective roles. Try this four-step process:

1. Let the staff know that you are the ultimate decider about your team's roles and accountability.

In the "Just Ask" leadership model, leaders should be willing to cede some control; however, "organizations are not democracies," says Bill McLaughlin, president & CEO of Select Comfort. Whenever possible, ask questions and allow coworkers the latitude to make their own decisions. In cases where you're going to make the final decision, make this clear in advance. Otherwise, coworkers who have gotten accustomed to being asked questions and making their own decisions will feel duped and betrayed.

2. Ask your coworkers to describe roles and lines of authority from their perspective. Ask the same of your boss. Then be sure that you fully understand the feedback you've received. If you're confused by someone's input, ask questions until you completely grasp that person's point of view. You need not agree with the other person's position, but you must communicate that you know the position and value the input.

3. Analyze any discrepancies in the responses you received. What roles or lines of authority are unclear? Why? Pay particular attention to how your role is defined by everybody. If your team comes to you with exceptions to the established rules, that may be because you aren't fully clear on your own role. Once you have processed all this information, present your findings, revised

roles, and new lines of authority (if needed) to your team.

4. In the future, when a coworker repeatedly comes in to discuss changes in sales territory, ask yourself: Am I the appropriate decider here? If you are, then you need to devise a better rule system so that your direct reports can handle these exceptions on their own in the future. If you are not the appropriate decider, then you need to make the organization's lines of authority clearer to your team.

Distribute as much authority as you can down the organization. In doing so, you're not abdicating responsibility; you're establishing it. At the same time, you must be clear about the decisions you alone will make and the process you will follow.

Ensure Accountability #8:

Am I an interrogator or an interviewer?

Law enforcement officers use interviews and interrogations to find out information from witnesses, victims, informants, and suspects. The difference between an interview and an interrogation is simple. Interrogations are meant to be stressful.

An interview ought to be conducted without stress. A stress-free environment isn't always easy to achieve, however. Tom Pritzker, CEO and chairman of Hyatt Corporation provides an example: Two attorneys walked into his office late one night and gravely intoned, "You have a problem!" Once the attorneys communicated the particulars of the crisis, Tom asked, "What solutions have you come up with?" "None," they answered. Some leaders would have let the attorneys' anxiety become their own. Not Tom. He asked the attorneys to brainstorm "What if?" scenarios and encouraged them not to dwell on negative outcomes. In doing so, he took the stress down to a manageable level, and pretty soon potential solutions arose. He'd created a safe environment, free from blame.

Interrogations take on a markedly different tone.

Dick Dunn, who ran one of the large airline reward programs for the Carlson Companies, experienced first-hand one of Curt Carlson's legendary interrogations. Curt, the founder and then CEO, got into the elevator with Dick and asked, "What is it that you do for me?" (It was a question he often asked.) Curt followed every question with another question, each more specific in nature: How much does a consumer consider a free ticket worth? How much does Northwest [Airlines] charge other companies, like hotel chains and long distance carriers, for each mile they purchase? How many miles do you earn for a flight between Minneapolis and Chicago? He drilled down to the angstrom (the finest measurement known to humans)—until, in other words, Dick no longer knew the answer.

That elevator ride seemed to take weeks, according to Dick. And it didn't end when the doors opened. Curt said that he would call in an hour to get the answer to the mileage question. Dick ran back to his office and frantically dug up the information. Sure enough, an hour went by and Curt called.

This story was recounted to me over a burger several years later. Not surprisingly, Dick doesn't recall it fondly. He felt ashamed for not knowing the answer in the elevator, and that shame stuck with him. He does, however, recall the exact number that Curt wanted that day—397.8 miles.

Stories of Curt's interrogations circulated throughout Carlson Companies. It wasn't so much the specific answers that Curt wanted, of course. He simply wanted to put everyone on notice: *You'd better know each and every aspect of your job. It's expected of you.* And they did.

Interrogations can be demeaning and stress inducing but effective at creating individual responsibility. Interviews create a spirit of teamwork and often lead to creative problem solving but may lead to slightly less preparedness. Is your organization's culture one of interrogations or interviews?

I prefer the interview culture, since it leads to a more harmonious work climate, but whichever culture you have, consistency matters a great deal. If you oscillate between the two, chances are that your coworkers will occasionally feel misled.

Ensure Accountability #9:

What am I afraid of losing?

According to researchers, fear of loss has a much greater psychological hold on people than the desire to gain. As we build our assets, our careers, and our accomplishments, we feel like they belong to us. With so many holdings, no wonder we feel more compelled to defend what we have than to take risks.

When our company went public, I monitored our market value in the morning newspaper or online. I couldn't believe how much I (and our company) was worth. I made my financial goal by age 36. As a result, I no longer felt the urge to slay the competition or defy convention; my goal became to protect what I'd already gained.

After challenging the status quo for years, our company became the status quo. The entire industry adopted our technological platform. In those heady days, I should have been looking for other revolutionary innovations. I should have been dangling my toes over the proverbial cliff's edge, but instead I concentrated on managing our growth. By the time I left, the company had begun its decline.

This desire to protect and defend can undo even the best of leaders. Ask yourself:

1. What am I afraid of losing?
2. Is this an illusion or real?

3. If I continue to defend, am I leading?

4. Is a defensive mindset serving me or the organization?

Not only do you have to overcome your own resistance to change, you likely have to overcome all your coworkers' resistance as well. After all, most people would rather stay with the known than suffer loss for the chance of something better.

If sharks don't move forward, they die. Keep fresh water moving through you and your organization. Don't sit and defend. Instead ask, "Can I afford not to take this risk?"

Ensure Accountability #10:

How do I give coworkers maximum latitude to make their own decisions?

Responsible for all operations and building maintenance at Moody Air Force Base, Col. Joseph Callahan is fond of telling his charges to "keep it between the rails." While that sounds like tough speak, it's actually quite liberating.

Imagine you're standing on railroad tracks, staring off into the distance. The tracks appear to get narrower as they near the horizon. The horizon, in Col. Callahan's metaphor, is the organization's goal. The rails of the tracks represent the organization's lines of authority and values, which shouldn't be crossed.

So when a member of his organization asks how to accomplish a specific project, and Col. Callahan responds, "It's up to you, but keep it between the rails," he's only placing two restrictions on the individual: respecting the organization's lines of authority and honoring its values. That leaves a lot of room for the team member to operate. At the same time, the process encourages his charges to keep an eye on the organization's goal.

While Lester Crown, chairman of Henry Crown and Company and former president and chairman of General Dynamics, shares Col. Callahan's convictions, he believes that not all coworkers deserve the same degree of latitude. Before you trust someone with the organization's crown jewels, in other words, he recommends that you gradually elevate the level of trust (and, thereby, the risk) associated with the project. Naturally, if the project were to hold no risk at all, it would be hard to evaluate the coworker's trustworthiness. But, provided the coworker passes each progressively risky task, trust will build—in both parties.

61

Trust must flow in both directions for it to be effective. If you communicate distrust to coworkers while simultaneously granting them freedom, your coworkers will have trouble determining how to act. They won't fully trust you and your proclamations of decision-making freedom. So don't assign a project unless you feel comfortable with the level of trust it demands.

By following Col. Joseph Callahan and Lester Crown's advice, you and your coworkers will make considerable progress down the tracks toward the organization's goal.

Ensure Accountability #11:

How can I reduce a coworker's fear of failure?

Maj. Gen. Dick Newton, who is responsible to the Secretary of the Air Force and Chief of Staff, introduced me to *Auftragstaktik* ("mission tactics"): a mission-oriented command process developed and employed by the German military in the early 1800s. Four key components are required for its success:

- Mutual trust among leaders based on each leader's intimate personal knowledge of the capabilities of the others.
- Training and organization in everything the army does to reinforce the primacy of the judgment of the man on the scene (decentralization).
- A willingness to act on the part of all leaders and those who aspire to be leaders.
- Simple, commonly accepted and understood operations concepts.

—Lieutenant Colonel John Silva (Baltic Defense College – Department of Operations April 1999 "*Auftragstaktik – Its Origin and Development*")

In the German military it was forgivable to act and have a poor outcome. It was, however, unforgivable not to act. With or without appropriate orders, the officer would be questioned afterward, but not interrogated. The focus of questioning would be to learn from the outcome, positive or negative. Retribution would break down the trust critical, culturally, to the success of the model. That's why the officer's superior was duty-bound to ensure that the questioning proceeded in a supportive manner.

The *Auftragstaktik* process recognized that split-second decisions on the battlefield could backfire but that indecision and paralysis were worse. And with the questioning process, officers could learn from mistakes, share strategies, and gain problem-solving insights without fear of recriminations or reprisal.

Fear of failure is, of course, directly related to fear of reprisal. Encourage your coworkers to act in the present, then reinforce your trust in them by concentrating on how future performance might be improved, no matter what the outcome.

Most of us associate the military with the command-and-control model of leadership. There are, of course, exceptions—like *Auftragstaktik* and Col. Callahan's "between the rails" model—which give individuals the latitude to make their own decisions and take risks.

Ensure Accountability #12:

When should I commit resources to new projects?

"Be careful what you wish for," the old saying goes. Instead, maybe it should be: "Be careful what you begin." Once you commence a project, you are—perhaps unwittingly—attaching yourself to a trajectory. If you're not careful, you may find yourself unable to hop off that trajectory, simply because you have invested too much time, money, and effort to accept failure.

Motorola found itself in such a position. They wanted to make consumer-based satellite phones, but after completing the first phase of their business plan (creating the technology), they realized they didn't have a viable marketing plan that would account for the high cost of delivery. Had they done so, they would have saved billions of dollars.

The following study, as it appeared in John Keith Murnighan's *Bargaining Games: A New Approach to Strategic Thinking in Negotiations*, indicates how psychologically attached we become to our failures.

> At the University of California at Berkeley, Barry Staw conducted several research projects investigating how commitment to a failed course of action can escalate.
>
> Business students read the fictitious case, which has had a long, profitable history but now appears in trouble. Acting as financial VPs, students are asked to invest $10 million in either the company's Consumer or Industrial products division.
>
> After they have made their decision, time is accelerated to five years later. Half of the VPs are told that their original decisions were successful: The division that received the extra funds had turned itself around and looked as if it would continue to be successful. The other VPs are told that

> their decisions were unsuccessful: The division that had
> received the influx of money was doing worse than ever.
> After this news, they must invest up to $20 million more in
> either of the two divisions, Consumer or Industrial products;
> this time they can divide the money any way they like.
>
> People whose previous decisions were unsuccessful
> pour more money into that same, failing division. Not only
> that, when they also face a serious personal threat (that is,
> losing their job), they commit even more to the unsuccess-
> ful division. Commitments do not escalate, however, when
> decision makers know that they will be throwing good
> money after bad. Only when they have hope of escaping
> the costs of previous poor decisions do decision makers
> escalate their commitments.

Instead of focusing on how to learn to cut your losses, let's address the issue on the front end: when should you escalate your commitment to new projects?

Here are some questions to ask in the early stages:

- Do you think future gains are possible, and what are the risks you would be willing to take for those gains?
- Is optimism blocking you from seeing negative consequences?
- Has the team overadvocated for the project, and do they now feel personally invested in, or identified with, the outcome?
- If faced with a worst-case scenario, would you still be able to walk away without a significant loss?

By the time you find yourself asking, "What propelled us to move in this direction to begin with?" it's usually too late to escape without disastrous, unimagined consequences. Save yourself the shame of having to admit your error by analyzing everyone's investment in the project at the outset, including your own.

Imagine worst-case scenarios and ask yourself, "How far are we willing to proceed before we cut our losses?"

Ensure Accountability Summary

To develop and maintain accountable coworkers, you must trust them and they must trust you.

Make the lines of authority clear, so that there is no confusion over decision-making responsibilities (especially if you are going to be the ultimate decision maker). Describe in detail the desired outcome, restrictions (or "rails"), and potential consequences and rewards. Be patient with your coworkers' pace of discovery, but address problematic behavior before it (and your frustration) becomes ingrained. Provided good-faith action was taken, make sure you learn from, and don't punish, failure.

As your coworkers demonstrate progress and initiative, provide them with progressively more challenging work and responsibilities. They will expect consistency on your part with regards to questioning style (interrogator or interviewer), enforcement of rules, and reactions to success and failure. If you ask and expect them to change and embrace change, you must be prepared to do so too.

You see things; and you say, "Why?"
But I dream things that never were; and I say,
  "Why not?"

—GEORGE BERNARD SHAW

CHAPTER 3

BUILD UNITY AND COOPERATION—CREATING A CULTURE OF TRUST

How can questions unify an organization made up of individuals with vastly different backgrounds, needs, and skills? Unity is no easy feat in this age of self-interest, but it's not impossible. As a leader, invite others to share their opinions. Listen well to your coworkers' responses and reflect back what you've heard. In doing so, your coworkers will know their opinions have been transmitted clearly—not transformed or colored by your own agenda. Treat questions from your coworkers as thoughtfully as you would have them treat yours and honor their independence, but connect their success to the organization as a whole. This approach will help you retain promising young leaders and handle star employees that aren't team-minded.

1. How can I liven up the "state of the organization" address?
2. If I have a better idea, should I share it with my team?
3. Why am I the only one who talks in meetings?
4. How can I get everyone to contribute?
5. How can storytelling build unity?
6. What are my team's needs?
7. How do I align each employee's needs with the needs of the organization?
8. Are you asking the right question but using the wrong tone?

9. What's the difference between *good* questions and *gotcha* questions?
10. How should I respond to good questions?
11. How can I be more present in conversations?
12. How do I show I am listening?
13. When should I seek advice from coworkers on my own work?
14. Why don't my coworkers come to me for advice?
15. What will it take to win over the people against me?
16. Can I trust my coworkers, and can they trust me?
17. Why are leaders leaving my organization?
18. How can I learn bad news sooner?
19. What can I do if a star employee constantly breaks the rules?

Build Unity and Cooperation #1:

How can I liven up the "state of the organization" address?

While it's important to take questions after you give a "state of the organization" address, you should ask questions, too. Give those in attendance a chance to shine. Let them provide answers or information that reveals their contributions to the organization.

It may seem counterintuitive that you, the leader, should do most of the asking. It's important to acknowledge and accept, however, that no leader can have all the answers. Acting as the "Oracle of Knowledge" can diminish your appeal and suggest that you're taking credit for the work of others. If you behave this way, your coworkers will relish occasions when you slip up, feel less inclination to achieve, and consider you an adversary, not a leader.

Try sending a copy of your presentation to each department (and any questions you have) prior to your organization-wide address, and ask the department heads for suggestions and comments. If you find their input particularly helpful or insightful, invite these leaders to conduct the presentation with you.

As a leader, it can be difficult to reduce your need to be the bearer of truth. The most successful leaders, though, are willing to be vulnerable, approachable, and open to others' perspectives. They know that questions empower others, build their own authority, and reveal information that might otherwise be overlooked.

Build Unity and Cooperation #2:

If I have a better idea, should I share it with my team?

Leaders typically have a greater sense of urgency than their coworkers. They also have a broader perspective and a greater range of experience. It's a dangerous mix.

In meetings, leaders have difficulty keeping quiet when they have an idea that's better than the ones currently being batted around. Revealing that idea, however, often spoils the learning and discovery process of their coworkers.

When coworkers are stuck, it makes sense for leaders to step in with questions that move them forward. But leaders shouldn't finish others' thoughts or provide their own solutions simply because they're impatient with the pace of discovery.

The damage inflicted on coworkers can be considerable, especially if they are emotionally charged by the discussion. When people link feelings and thinking, there exists the possibility for real and permanent change. If leaders disrupt this process, nobody is well served.

A client of mine runs a distribution business in the Northeast. She wanted to process-map her entire organization, systematize each step, and then provide it to her coworkers so that they would make fewer errors. In essence, she wanted to provide them with her great idea.

Which process would resonate more with you?

1. "I've put together a process map and instructions for you to do your job without errors. I would like you to review this, make minor changes if necessary, and implement it at once."

2. "We've been experiencing too many errors in our production area. Can you devise a plan to ensure 99.5 percent error-free production and implement those changes?"

Most people would choose process 2, and so should you. If you're uncomfortable relinquishing all control to your coworkers, ask them for their recommendation before they implement it. This will provide you with an opportunity to ask questions that test their ability to meet the goal.

The only thing that truly matters is that the work gets done to meet the objective, on time and budget—not that your coworkers reach the same decisions you did.

Your coworkers' process might not be as efficient as yours (on paper), but in practice the implementation of their plan will be faster—simply because the person implementing the idea was the one who came up with it.

Build Unity and Cooperation #3:

Why am I the only one who talks at meetings?

If you think you're talking too much at meetings, so does everyone else.

Some leaders believe that if they aren't controlling others, then they themselves are being controlled. They approach meetings as if they're tug-of-war contests. Instead, they should see meetings as an exchange of information and ideas. They should seize these opportunities to ask questions, not bludgeon others with their opinions.

Mike Harper, former CEO and chairman of ConAgra, always opened meetings with a question. He then sat forward and listened to everyone's problem-solving ideas. If he noticed that someone wasn't speaking much, he would invite that person to contribute. Mike would be encouraging and supportive even when his coworker's comments were not on track with his agenda. By providing heavy doses of support over the course of five or six meetings, Mike could usually draw this coworker out to be a fully functioning part of the team. If this coworker continued to be withdrawn, however, Mike made it clear that he or she would have to move on.

Sometimes you can have too much of a good thing. When Mike encountered a coworker who talked too much in meetings, he applied a different strategy. Careful to avoid belittling this person in front of others, Mike would direct his next question at someone else or use a nonverbal gesture (like the sweep of his arm) that emphasized his desire to hear from others.

A team often needs leadership rather than just consensus. Mike's approach still provided leadership. If someone began guiding the discussion away from the company's visions, goals, objectives, and values, Mike would simply ask, "How does this help us meet our goal?" or, "Is this in alignment with our vision?"

Mike had a motto, which he taught to everyone, including me: "E^3: Earnings, Earnings, Earnings." An analyst once asked Mike about his goals for the company. Mike's answer was simply, "Earnings." When asked if he had other goals, Mike said, "Oh, yes. Our second goal is earnings, and our third goal is earnings." When Mike asked, "How does this help us meet our goal?" in meetings, everyone understood exactly what he meant.

If you want to see innovation in your company, follow Mike's example: ask a question, then be silent and listen. Books on leadership speak much about courage. It takes courage to trust your team. It takes courage to believe your coworkers will deliver ideas and execute them successfully. Chances are, though, that they will—if you give them space, encouragement, and a clear goal.

75

Build Unity and Cooperation #4:
How can I get everyone to contribute?

"It was their idea. I don't even know who even suggested it, but everyone loved it." Mike Broderick, CEO and founder of Turning Technologies, said this when describing how his company came up with the name for its new product: Response Card.

Mike received 60 suggestions for a product name from his coworkers. They then used the Ranking Wizard (a great feature of TurningPoint software, a principal product of Turning Technologies) to rate these suggestions based on three criteria:

1. The product's applications
2. Memorableness
3. Likability

The top eight to ten suggestions were rated again. The name Response Card rose to the top, and everyone felt committed to it—mostly because they had a hand in the decision-making process.

In *The Wisdom of Crowds*, James Surowiecki explains how the aggregate view of a group is more likely to obtain a better answer than any single member of that group. Turning Technologies takes that thinking and applies it to organizational settings, like PowerPoint presentations.

Imagine that when you asked your coworkers a question in the middle of a presentation, they used a small remote control to register their responses, and you received an aggregate response immediately. With this TurningPoint feature, not only are you virtually assured of coworkers staying awake and alert, but lectures will become dynamic questioning sessions with a much higher probability of changing opinions and reaching consensus—in part because the process can preserve anonymity. Your coworkers don't have to raise their hands sheepishly after looking to see how everyone else, especially you (the leader), is voting.

If your organization has grown as much as Turning Technologies (now with more than 90 employees), building unity and cooperation can be difficult. Try using technology that allows everyone's voice to be heard. Trust the wisdom of the crowd, not only to come up with ideas but also to evaluate them.

Build Unity and Cooperation #5:
How can storytelling build unity?

Surely the shortest distance between setting a goal and achieving it is a command, right? Like the Nike slogan says: Just do it.

Not necessarily. Not if the goal is to inspire or unite your troops. Commands might unite your troops against you, but rarely is the converse true. To create a cohesive group, use questions that evoke shared experiences and stories. When people tell stories, they reveal their strengths and weaknesses. These stories trigger emotions that prompt listeners to consider similar stories in their own lives. Pretty soon, the group forms a collective identity around their shared experiences, language, and values. Individuals then make this group identity part of their own.

This storytelling/bonding phenomenon goes by many names, one of them being *fantasy theme analysis*, after a study by Ernest G. Bormann in *Discussion and Group Methods* (Harper & Row, 1969). He discovered that people galvanize more around emotional stories than

syllogisms or scientific experiments. "We are not necessarily persuaded by reason," Bormann said. "We are
often persuaded by suggestion that ties in with our
dreams."

TV advertisements know all about this power to suggest. Commercials seldom try to persuade you to buy a
product with logic. Instead, they craft little parables that
sweep you away in a tide of emotion. The pickup truck,
splashing through the mud, is the embodiment of freedom in America. The cell phone commercial reminds you
that you have 100 percent coverage because an army of
tele-dweebs is out there checking every square inch of
real estate: "Can you hear me now?"

If you want to use stories to create excitement and
cohesion in your organization, ask questions that stir the
common feelings of coworkers:

- What have we done together in the past that
  helped us overcome what seemed like
  insurmountable obstacles?
- How can we change the world?
- What makes us feel good when we come to work?
- What values are present when you have a great
  day at work?
- If you could be in charge for one day, what would
  you like to see happen?

Phil Condit, former CEO and chairman of Boeing,
united workers at Boeing under the phrase "working
together" as they designed and manufactured a new

plane, the 777. The phrase was particularly apt because Boeing engineers were asked to team with production people for the first time. The "working together" slogan extended to suppliers, too, who needed to be embraced in order for Boeing to produce a plane with over 4 million individual parts.

Poet and organizational philosopher David Whyte calls leaders the "chief conversationalists." He believes leaders should think not of what they have to do but of what conversations need to take place. Whyte recalled being at a Boeing site where someone had crossed out the word *working* on a banner and written something underneath. "I went over to look at the banner because I thought it would give me a real insight towards what was really going on," said Whyte. "But instead of something scurrilous there, I was startled to see the word *imagining*. I thought: what a good sign that they were talking about imagining together."

A group can be downcast, even despairing, but the moment they are asked to create a goal for themselves, their dynamic undergoes a huge change. Instead of *you* talking, *they* are talking. They're interested. They're involved. Their egos and ownership drive kick in, and when that happens, the quality of their responses elevates.

What are we here for? What are the limits? Who are we? These questions charge people's souls and invite them to consider all possibilities. See what common stories emerge; then use them to create, hone, or reinforce a group identity.

79

Build Unity and Cooperation #6:

What are my team's needs?

The Golden Rule says, "Do unto others as they would do unto you." After witnessing selfish or cruel acts, parents put their hands on their children's shoulders and speak these words in grave tones—and for good reason. The Golden Rule prompts us to ask, "What if the situation were reversed?" The act of imagining another's perspective helps to build cooperation and generosity, which is why the Golden Rule has withstood the test of time. The problem is, too often we don't know what others really want!

My parents live in Scottsdale, Arizona, where they observed a homeless woman, dressed in rags, scouring a dumpster for her breakfast. When she extracted a large unopened box of donuts, a passerby yelled, "Wow, this is your lucky day!" The woman responded, "What do you mean my 'lucky day'? I can't eat these." She tossed the box back in. "I'm watching my weight."

We can get into trouble when we make assumptions about what others want. I often hear leaders say, "They should be so grateful for what we're doing for them. If I were in their position, this is exactly what I would want for myself." True, but it may not be what their coworkers want or need.

Early in our business, Rick Diamond and I wanted to provide our staff with health insurance. Since we'd received some requests for pay increases, we put it to a vote: pay increase or health insurance? Due to the margins in our industry, we couldn't afford both. To our amazement, our staff opted for the pay increase. If we hadn't asked for their input, we would have acted paternally and chosen the health insurance option because we would have slept better knowing that all our employees were covered. But, ultimately, we wouldn't have given them what they really wanted.

Hillel, a rabbinic scholar and philosopher, modified the Golden Rule. His version reads: "Do unto others as they would have done unto themselves." This prompts leaders to ask, "What are my coworkers' unique needs and desires, and how can I help meet them?"

Survey your staff on a regular basis. What are their unique needs and desires? Search not only for answers to this question but also for the rationales. In asking, "For what reason?" you will get a much better sense of what drives your coworkers.

Build Unity and Cooperation #7:

How do I align each employee's needs with the needs of the organization?

We have more individual choices than ever. We can choose from 16 movies at a megaplex, eight different kinds of orange juice (low acid, lots of pulp, not from concentrate, and so on), and countless shoe brands and styles. Is it any surprise that we want to be free to make choices in our jobs as well?

If you grew up with only four TV channels to choose from, you might believe that command-style leadership is still viable. You might believe in shared values and needs, the way some people did in the 1960s. Unfortunately, centralized leadership doesn't work with the current generation. People want to work *their* way, not *your* way. They know what motivates them and how they best achieve results and obtain information, and they want to receive full credit for their efforts. If you try to steamroll their independence, you'll wind up with flattened cartoon characters, not productive employees.

As a leader today, you must decentralize power and authority. With leadership opportunities, your coworkers will find personal meaning in the work they do. And they'll do it well, provided you meet their needs. Your challenge—accommodating leaders on all levels of the organization—is daunting, maybe even terrifying. How do you align everyone's needs with the needs of the organization? With so many leaders, so much independence, will chaos be far behind?

Not necessarily. Not if you build in some safeguards. It's important to understand that total independence is often desired but not always healthy. Individuality is good, but individualism can lead to a sense of helplessness, and this helplessness can lead to depression. Despite fiercely independent childhood heroes like Superman, Batman, and Wonder Woman, we want and need to be part of something greater than ourselves. We want the support of a community.

We want to feel like the work we do has meaning, not only to ourselves but also to others. Chances are, this meaning has already been established—in the form of your organization's founding mission, vision, goals, and values. These pillars were originally set by the founder and then enhanced through time by the organization's leadership teams. As a leader, you can bring this meaning to your coworkers by frequently asking how their needs and goals match the organization's. In doing so, you give them the respect they want and need, as well as communicate a sense of belonging to a larger community.

Do you believe in your organization's mission, vision, goals, and values? If so, you'll be able to impart this sense of togetherness to your charges. If not, you'll be herding cats.

Authentic leadership requires allowing everyone to lead at times but to instill one cohesive purpose so that these leaders will work together and move in one over-arching direction. For each and every project, ask yourself, "How does this contribute to our organization's mission, vision, goals, and values?" Ask the same of your direct reports. And have them ask the same of their direct reports.

Build Unity and Cooperation #8:

Are you asking the right question but using the wrong tone?

My wife, Chris, is an executive recruiter and can read people and animals with uncanny ability. We were running along a lake recently and she said, "Libby [our dog] needs to go into the water." The second I unleashed Libby, she bolted to the water and sat relaxing and lapping up the water as only a dog can.

Two female police officers parked close by. "Do you think we did something wrong?" Chris asked. "I don't think so," I responded.

As the police officers approached, one asked, "Do you have ID?" That question could have been asked with a casual disarming tone, especially since Chris and I were wearing running clothes with no pockets—a fact that I doubt was lost on the officers. Instead, the tone was threatening and intense—more of a demand than a question.

The officers explained that an unleashed dog was a $175 fine. Allowing the dog in the water was an additional $175 fine. "Are you really going to give us a ticket for this?" I asked, upset. I repeated the question, in a more demure tone, trying to communicate to the officers that I wasn't a threat to them or their power. Finally, one of them said, "No."

Police officers and federal agents are often fearful when approaching suspects. It pays for them to be wary, take precautions, and project strength. But they ought to tailor their tone based upon the setting and situation. If they don't, they may incite conflict, not avoid it.

When asking a question, consider your tone. Can you detect a hint of power, arrogance, sarcasm, indifference, or cynicism? Can others? If so, it doesn't matter how good a question you ask.

If you ask, "What can I do to help you complete this project on time?" but your tone suggests impatience and irritation, your coworker will sense the underlying feelings and likely respond defensively or refuse your offer. You may feel like you've been fair and upheld your responsibilities, but you really haven't. Your tone and your questions sent conflicting messages.

Tones are imprinted in us from childhood, long before we understood the signposts that symbolic language provides. Make sure the tone and meaning of your words are in sync. When you ask a question, think not only of what you want to say but also of which tone you want to use.

85

Build Unity and Cooperation #9:

What's the difference between *good* questions and *gotcha* questions?

Good questions are both challenging and inviting. They house the potential for growth and collaboration. They are delivered with enthusiasm and don't carry judgment or firm guidance. The destination is left wide open.

You're unlikely to get a cursory answer from a good question. If you're lucky, you might get a "Good question!" in return. When you do, it's often because responders want to support your inquiry, but also give themselves additional time to consider their response.

Gotcha questions will sometimes elicit a "Good question!" from responders, too, but there's nothing good about them. These are questions geared toward making others look bad—and elevate the asker in the process.

According to Ron James, president and CEO of the Center for Ethical Business Cultures, boardrooms are notorious havens for gotcha questions. In a room full of prestigious CEOs, newcomers have to demonstrate why they're worthy of being in this group, and one way to do that is by asking questions that people can't answer. The result, says James, is that other board members think, "Well, I'd better come up with a question that can stump the rest, too." Pretty soon the spirit of the board—a space where leaders ought to be allowed to feel and express vulnerability, and collect wisdom from others—is violated. Members are concerned about not looking foolish, so they withhold questions or answers, and the quality of their work suffers.

Don't let your ego get the best of you. Don't ask questions that undermine the good, collective efforts of others.

Build Unity and Cooperation #10:

How should I respond to good questions?

My fourth-grade teacher stood before us and said, "Class, I want you to understand that it's not the answer that's important, but the question." It was as if an angel had floated down on a cloud and handed me a golden truth. I knew that this statement was *major*. For one shining moment, I was in love with Mrs. Middleschmidt.

She then revealed her question: "Class, can anyone tell me where Colorado is on the map?"

My ardor for Mrs. Middleshmidt dissipated into the chalk dust. I love Colorado, but neither that question nor the answer was *important*.

People often give lip service to the importance of questions but then proceed to ask closed-ended questions (like the Colorado question). Or they appreciate questions—just so long as they're the ones asking them. As a leader, you have an obligation not only to ask open-ended questions but also to welcome ones asked of you.

Rather than give credit for good questions, we sometimes take a defensive posture—out of tiredness, embarrassment (for not knowing the answer), or fear of encouraging more questions. We are reminded of children asking question after question ("What are you doing?" "What's that for?" "Who's your best friend?" "If you don't like doing that, why do you do it?"). Eventually, questions grow tiresome, even if we love and respect our audience. So, sometimes we shut off questions before they get a chance to annoy us ("That's a stupid question").

And yet questions come so naturally to us. They help us make the right decisions. They help us lead organizations. They help us stay on track. They move us from being stuck to being wonderfully unstuck.

People hail you like a conquering hero if you come up with a great answer. But if you come up with a great question, where's the ticker-tape parade?

Applaud those who ask you good, important questions. And be prepared to answer those that are asked of you.

Build Unity and Cooperation #11:

How can I be more present in conversations?

"You don't need to know what you're going to ask next if you really listen to what the person is saying," said Bob Aronson, press secretary to former Minnesota governor Rudy Perpich and highly sought after communication coach. Questions naturally rise to the surface if you're engaged in the conversation. Veteran reporters know this phenomenon to be true. During an interview, they don't need to consult a list of questions. They just listen and the questions come effortlessly.

During comedy improvisations, the actors must riff off everything their partners say—without the benefit of a safety net. With lots of practice, they learn to keep the comedy and conversation moving forward, not stagnating. Their exercises are geared toward thinking and reacting quickly while listening intently. Here's an example of an improv exercise for you to try with a partner:

1. Each person thinks of a story (how a car pulled out of a parking space and knocked over your grocery cart) or a set of instructions (how to make a pumpkin pie).
2. Face each other and tell your story or set of instructions simultaneously. Use hand gestures and vary your tone to get the other person's attention.
3. While you are each carrying on your monologue (for roughly two minutes), listen to what your partner is saying.
4. When you're done with your monologues, try to recall exactly what your partner said.

Improv comedy bombs when one or both of the actors don't react to what is said and instead say something they've been preparing to say. These contributions don't sound natural and aren't usually funny because they don't stem organically from the conversation. And, if one actor doesn't build off a partner's contribution to the conversation, the partner might get irritated. Pretty soon, the actors are competing against each other, not carrying the comedy together. This is why one of the foundational rules of improv is never to say "No" and shut down a partner's attempt to take the conversation in a new direction. Partners must work in the spirit of cooperation; otherwise, their exchange will run dry.

Leaders often think they know what a person is going to say, stop listening, and begin forming their next question before the talker is finished. Like an ace reporter or successful improv actor, stay with the conversation and listen to all the nuances. Don't drift off, and, by all means, don't take an adversarial posture. If you do either, the talker won't want to help you accomplish your goals. The exchange will run dry.

If your responses flow organically from the conversation, your coworkers will feel affirmed and engaged. And if you're listening closely, you'll recognize the difference between "We should be able to meet that objective" and "We will meet that objective." Picking up on these nuances can mean the difference between success and failure.

If polled, most leaders would say they're great multitaskers. They may think they are, but most people can't actually do two things effectively at the same time. What most people claim is multitasking is really doing two things and moving between these tasks. How many times have you been on the phone and been annoyed when the other person is clearly working on the computer or reading something instead of focusing on the conversation? When you hang up the phone, do you feel like you've really been heard?

Stay with the conversation. Stay present. The questions will come naturally.

Build Unity and Cooperation #12:
How do I show I am listening?

The consensus among leaders is that listening to the answer is more important than asking the perfect question. Unfortunately, listening is fast becoming a lost art. According to Tom Madison, former president of US West Communications, "Young people, in particular, don't know how to listen. They are taught in college to listen for facts, but not what lies behind the facts."

Listening intently will allow you to grasp the motivation behind the facts. It will also build trust between you and the speaker. Keep that in mind as you implement these three tips to improve your listening:

1. *Don't let your mind wander.* Zen masters can keep their minds completely focused on one thought or conversation, but most of us can't. We might, for instance, latch onto one piece of information that the speaker has said. We grip it tightly and plan our response, rather than simply book-marking this information and continuing to listen. The speaker will sense our disengagement. Trust, confidence, and motivation will dip. Rather than hold onto one point, open yourself

up to many others. Even if you forget the point you initially wanted to make, if you stay focused on listening you'll likely discover several other ways to propel the conversation forward.

2. *Be patient.* Leaders often have Type A personalities, so they want to complete others' sentences. Instead of interrupting, allow coworkers adequate time to speak and ask questions. Doctors at the renowned Mayo Clinic in Rochester, Minnesota, pride themselves on patience. They know that people can be reluctant to reveal personal, sometimes embarrassing information. Mayo doctors listen to their patients' questions and "seemingly unrelated" information that might prove critical to reaching a correct diagnosis or customized treatment plan. Good doctors and good leaders have patience and make better decisions as a result. They listen to what is said, not what they believe will be said.

3. *Don't ask a question and then give an answer to see if you were right.* I was in a coaching exercise with a CEO who summoned his accountant and asked, "What are our revenue and net profits going to be this year?" Before she could answer, he said, "$5 million and $1 million, respectively." He clearly wanted to demonstrate to me and to her that he was aware of the numbers. This performance was about ego, and it did nothing to build his leadership. What's the accountant's

incentive to try to answer that man's questions in the future? Wasn't he communicating that her time must not be valuable if she was going to be called into the office just so he could ask and answer his own question? Does she now think he has nothing better to do with his time? Actually, these aren't assumptions. This is what I discovered when I spoke with her afterward.

If you stay present in the conversation, are patient, and demonstrate respect for others, you'll be a good listener. And you'll be pleasantly surprised to find out how prepared your coworkers are for their meetings with you.

Build Unity and Cooperation #13:

When should I seek advice from coworkers on my own work?

Leaders can be terrific question askers when it comes to helping others, but when it comes to their own work they can be tight-lipped and territorial. They may stubbornly refuse help.

In a national survey conducted by CO2 Partners, we asked employees, "How often does your boss ask for your advice on solving a problem at work?" Here's what they said:

- Seldom/Never 32.6%

- Often/Occasionally 62.6%
- Don't know 3.9%

Despite a nationwide trend toward increasing team-work and maximizing individual contributions, roughly a third of the workforce isn't allowed to flex their problem-solving muscles. What are leaders afraid of? Too many good ideas? How many of these same leaders, do you think, claim to be striving for higher employee engagement?

Being asked to contribute a suggestion is a sign of regard. That should be reason enough to ask for input.

Unfortunately, if the survey question had asked about solving an "important" problem, I suspect the results would have been even more demoralizing. Too often leaders trust only themselves when the stakes are high, resulting in less input and greater employee alienation.

Among the other findings:

- Women are somewhat less likely than men (30.8 percent versus 34.7 percent) to be asked for input by an employer.
- The less education an employee has, the less likely he or she will be asked to contribute an idea. Forty percent of those with a high school diploma (or less education) reported seldom or never being asked for advice, compared to just 20.9 percent of college graduates.
- Likewise, 45.7 percent of employees earning less than $25,000 annually reported seldom or never

being consulted, compared with just 24.7 percent of those earning more than $75,000.

- There were no significant differences among age groups.

The survey findings reflect top-down bias. How foolish to think that only the most educated or highest-ranking employees are worthy of being consulted! Less-educated workers are often the most involved in product production and communicating with customers. They're the ones I'd want to talk with first.

I would caution you against asking questions if you aren't genuinely prepared to listen to responses, however. If you don't show respect for input, the quality of responses will decline over time—"validating" your reluctance to ask questions in the first place.

Build Unity and Cooperation #14:

Why don't my coworkers come to me for advice?

Employees should look to their supervisors for work-related advice, but only 11 percent do, according to an Internet survey I conducted of 3,000 employees.

The bottom line is that supervisors can't be trusted.

This lack of trust can be traced to four sources. First, supervisors are responsible for evaluating their employees' performance. As such, employees (especially if they're relatively high up in the organization) don't want to reveal weakness or ignorance to their immediate superiors. After all, this information could wind up on their performance reviews.

Second, organizational leaders don't do a good enough job of revealing their own weaknesses and knowledge gaps. Unless leaders do this—repeatedly, convincingly, and authentically—their coworkers won't come to them for advice. It's just too much of a professional risk.

Third, supervisors emit signals, if not outright statements, that they are too busy to be bothered. They might also unreasonably expect their employees to be completely self-reliant or to already know all the answers.

Last, supervisors simply might be adhering to the organizational culture dictated by their bosses or employers (i.e., everyone for themselves). In this case, supervisors are simply passing the distrust down the line.

If you want your coworkers to come to you rather than to seek counsel from peers, spouses, other senior partners, friends, or (worst of all) no one, prove that you are worthy of their trust. Make it clear that mistakes or knowledge gaps are opportunities for improvement, not signs of weakness. Not only do questions open dialogue, they increase efficiency (by enabling the asker to avoid pointless pursuits). Instill in your coworkers the following message: *to ask a question is to take responsibility*.

Build Unity and Cooperation #15:

What will it take to win over the people against me?

Not everyone in your organization will support you or your position all of the time. Even if your organization consists of only two people, you're bound to run into disagreement. So, for important undertakings, ask yourself:

- Who has a stake in this matter?
- Are they strongly on board?
- Are they on board?
- Are they against me?

Focus on the ones against you. Don't dismiss them as lunatics, misanthropes, or idiots—as tempting as that response might be. And don't expect them to be hit with "The Light" and get into line behind you. It's up to you to build support for your leadership and address their concerns (e.g., unmet needs, lack of recognition or opportunities, perceived slights).

Try GPSing. Your *goal* is to gain their support. Your *position* is that they are against you, but why? Your *strategy* will depend upon their reason(s). You might have to convince them that the good of the group is more important than the good of the individual, make a concession on an issue that's important to them, or hash out an agreement that involves compromise on both parts.

I know a vice president in a large multinational corporation who wants to be promoted to general management but who has been blocked by several coworkers, including his own boss. Questions helped him identify the obstacles to his promotion:

- What is it that they don't see in me?
- What competencies are they looking for me to develop?
- What social networks might I have alienated, and why?

Try as he might, he still couldn't grasp the rationale behind his boss's position. After all, this VP had always performed well. He'd made himself virtually indispensable. That was it! His boss had no reason to object to his promotion on worthiness grounds. It was self-interest that kept his boss from supporting the promotion. He couldn't bear losing this VP!

The people against you aren't going to help you—sometimes not even in identifying the reason(s) why they're against you. It's up to you to build the bridge across.

If you're unable to bridge the gap between you and your adversaries, consider the opposite approach: an ultimatum. Select Comfort was one month away from bankruptcy when Bill McLaughlin took over the top job. He didn't have the luxury of time to woo his critics over; this was the company's last shot at financial solvency. He wanted to position Select Comfort as the "Sleep Number" company. He needed everyone on his top team to commit to that branding message. They had to be willing to bet their jobs on it. In a meeting with the senior team, he announced that anyone not in alignment with the company's new direction should see him after the meeting to discuss severance packages. Two people took him up on the offer. The rest stayed. Whatever objections they had were automatically weakened by their decision to remain with the company.

Do you know who the stakeholders are? Do you know where you stand with them? Why are some people against you? What do you need to do to win their support? Answer these questions and your undertakings will have a much higher degree of success.

Build Unity and Cooperation #16:

Can I trust my coworkers, and can they trust me?

"You don't have to be alone to feel lonely."

—Ziggy

Richard Gelb, one-time CEO at Bristol-Myers Squibbs, had two assistants just to maintain his schedule. As a leader, you may not have two assistants, but your schedule is likely booked anywhere from two weeks to three months in advance. Your day begins with people and it's go, go, go from there. Coworkers trail you out the door at the end of the day, still eager for your input and attention.

You go home, expecting to breathe a little easier, but your kids want to play and your partner wants to exchange stories. In many ways, your mind is busier than it was at work, since you're interacting with family members and simultaneously trying to solve residual work-related issues.

When your family goes to bed, you head to your home office. Your mind is tired, but you're finally by yourself. So, why do you feel such a profound loneliness? How could that be when you've had people around you all day and you've been itching to escape their requests and questions? According to many leaders, loneliness seeps in because they feel the responsibility to solve not only their problems but everyone else's as well. It's a loneliness borne from decision making and lack of trust.

Mary Brainerd, CEO of HealthPartners, rarely feels alone in her work as a leader. She trusts her team and naturally speaks in "we" language, not "I," even when pushed to take credit for an idea. When asked if she ever goes home at night with her mind reeling from a seemingly unsolvable work-related problem, she responded, "No. The problems of this organization have 9,000 people working towards solutions daily." The successes and failures of HealthPartners rest on all of the employees, so Mary sleeps easily.

If you want more separation between your private and work lives, and if you, too, want to sleep easily, first answer the following questions:

- Do you trust all of your direct reports to solve tough problems?

- Do you trust all of your staff with your career?

If you can't answer these questions with a resounding yes, then either you haven't given your coworkers a chance to earn your trust or some of them simply aren't trustworthy.

In order to have followers on whom you can rely, you must first have the courage to trust them. By "trust," I mean not just to follow your directions but also to use their judgment, creativity, and critical thinking to solve issues on their own or with their team.

Here are a few questions to test your trust level in coworkers:

- Do you bypass certain coworkers with important projects?
- Do you only have a few coworkers in your circle of trust?
- Do you often say or think, "It would be quicker to do this myself," rather than delegate the project to the appropriate coworker?

For your own peace of mind, you must put your career in the hands of your coworkers. Teams only work when there is complete trust among all members—both upward and downward in the organization. If you can't trust certain coworkers, you're at risk of doing their jobs. In the process, you will wind up carrying their problems, leading to sleepless nights. Plus, if you don't trust one of your coworkers, then it is likely that the rest of the team won't either. Lack of trust leads to gossip and triangulating conversations. Naturally, you'll want to distance yourself from these cancerous activities. In doing so, you'll isolate yourself from everyone, not just the coworker you don't trust.

If you don't trust a coworker, you have two options: (1) learn what it is about this coworker that you don't trust and work toward a resolution or (2) move him or her out and bring in someone you and the team can trust.

There is no point assigning work to people you can't trust. After all, you won't believe in the answers they provide. The more you trust your coworkers and they prove worthy of that trust, the more the loneliness and sleeplessness will recede.

Build Unity and Cooperation #17:

Why are leaders leaving my organization?

Scott, a close friend of mine, served as chair of the education committee at a local synagogue. When we go out for monthly sushi, he's usually upbeat. That wasn't the case, though, when the head of the education program resigned and the rabbi hired a temporary replacement without first consulting Scott.

A week later, Scott brought up the issue of governance and the rabbi's executive decision at the board meeting.

The board thought it was more important, however, to discuss another member's trip to Africa. Scott left feeling unappreciated, ill-used, and unheard.

What did the rabbi do wrong? Perhaps nothing from a line-of-authority standpoint. She must have felt empowered by the board to make such decisions, and the board's confirmation signaled that she was correct. From a leadership standpoint, however, she failed. She could have easily involved Scott in the process. All she needed to do was ask, "Scott, what do you think we should do about this?" or "Scott, I have an opportunity to hire a temporary replacement until we have time to really go out and do a search. How do you think I should handle it?" Instead, she conveyed the following unspoken messages: "Scott, you're not really needed here" and "I don't really value your input."

Scott is a highly educated and hugely successful attorney. Any board would hunger for his decision-making ability. People pay a lot of money for his counsel, and he was willing to give it away for free.

Sadly, Scott decided his time was better spent elsewhere. He is no longer an active participant in the synagogue's leadership. And, in all likelihood, the rabbi will continue to make executive decisions without first consulting others.

If you want the leaders in your organization to make making meaningful contributions, let them. If you don't, they'll go somewhere they can.

Build Unity and Cooperation #18:
How can I learn bad news sooner?

Mark Feil, a senior vice president at Global Crossing during its boom time, appreciates great questions, but he cares more about what leaders do with the answers they receive. Do they see answers as an opportunity to gain better awareness of the organization's culture, processes, and individuals? Or do they see them as an opportunity to lay blame?

Mark recalled a time when a senior executive at Global Crossing asked an assembly of customer service reps, "What can we do better?" One rep said that the recent merger of five companies (all involved in telecommunications) had created some logistical problems. When this executive pressed for the name of a particular department that had performed badly, the rep reluctantly complied. The executive then got the head of the provisioning department on speaker phone. He did a "fly by"—chewing the provisioning department head out in front of the others, then quickly leaving.

Imagine the fallout. The head of the provisioning department was now ashamed and upset about being called out publicly (and unexpectedly) by the CEO. Do you think the customer service rep escaped without repercussions? No way.

Yes, the executive likely spurred the provisioning department to improve its work in the short term, but he did so at the expense of intracompany harmony.

You can ask the best questions in the world, but if you betray trust by sharing answers inappropriately—even once—you won't get good, honest feedback in the future.

If you want to hear bad news sooner, don't engage in public shaming. Prove that you're not only listening but also handling feedback responsibly.

Build Unity and Cooperation #19:

What can I do if a star employee constantly breaks the rules?

If your star employee doesn't respect the rules, he or she may be an "organizational terrorist." Organizational terrorists are aware of their power and use it to hold others hostage. Naturally, organizational terrorists shouldn't be confused with car-bombing terrorists or the perpetrators of the attacks on September 11, 2001, but they don't care if they do harm so long as their desires are met.

Before confronting an organizational terrorist, ask yourself, "How did this happen?" Search for the root cause. Ask, "Is this behavior regularly tolerated?" Enron's CEO learned that two traders were stealing from the company, but he did nothing to stop it. These traders were very profitable, after all. The CEO's lack of action implied that, if you were bringing in enough money, you, too, could steal.

In the process of establishing the root cause, you must look frankly at your own practices. If you determine that you were complicit with the situation, find a coach or mentor to help build boundaries with your team. Without making changes, you likely will face this issue again.

Next, focus your attention on the star employee. Ask yourself:

1. Is the employee capable of learning?
2. Do I have the time and resources available to train this employee?
3. Is the employee motivated to learn and change? (Note: Organizational terrorists often are not motivated to change since they are usually highly productive at their jobs.)

If the answer is yes to all three, then start the training program immediately. If the answer to any of these questions is no, then the decision of whether to fire or train is simple. As Donald Trump would say, "You're fired!"

Since firing this employee could compromise the company's strategic direction, you should seek the advice of other leaders in your organization, including those at the highest level. It's important to recognize the magnitude of your decision; after all, diminished revenue (as a result of the departure of the organizational terrorist) may mean having to fire others, not just this employee.

When meeting with other leaders, tell them the steps you have taken and ask these strategic questions:

1. At what point are we willing to take a principled stance on the issue, despite lost revenue?
2. How will our decision affect other employees?
3. Will we need to make cuts to compensate for the loss of revenue?
4. How will our decision affect the industry?
5. If this employee is fired, will she go to work for a competitor?
6. What impact could this have?

By working with others to answer these questions, their feelings of problem ownership should increase and complaints directed at you should decrease. From my experience, I foresee your team developing a plan that resembles the following:

Part A: Continue coaching the employee.
Part B: Build the rest of the staff in order to reduce dependence on the employee.
Part C: Start seeking a replacement.

Through all of this, make sure your team knows you're coaching the employee and that his behavior is not being tolerated. It's inappropriate to say anything more about this employee. Taking these steps will build your credibility as a leader. And your organization will need strong leadership to avoid the creation of a terrorist cell and to stay upbeat after the loss of the star employee.

Build Unity and Cooperation Summary

If you don't reduce your need to be the bearer of truth, your coworkers may start to see you as an adversary, depart for more meaningful job opportunities, and leave you to crumble under the weight of too much responsibility. Instead of pushing your ideas and actions, concentrate instead on the conversations that need to take place. Trust the wisdom of others (the crowd especially), provided it aligns with the organization's mission and values. Ask good and important questions (not gotcha questions) of everyone, not just your inner circle, and reinforce these respectful questions with the proper tone. Listen to what is said, not what you believe will be said, and handle this feedback responsibly.

No problem can be solved from the same consciousness that created it.
We must learn to see the world anew.

—ALBERT EINSTEIN

CHAPTER 4

CREATE BETTER DECISIONS—GETTING THE RIGHT ANSWERS BY ASKING THE RIGHT QUESTIONS

When should you entrust decisions to others? This chapter is divided into three sections (context, clarity, and objectivity) to give a sense of how environment, conflicting information, and biases can influence decision making. If you don't routinely ask, "Whose decision is it?" you'll fall into the trap of doing others' work. The more jobs you try to do, the more likely you'll fail or die of exhaustion. Learn how to direct decision making to the appropriate party, seek clarification, and provide solutions when appropriate. If you want accountable coworkers, you must hold yourself accountable for not overstepping your bounds.

Context

1. Whose decision is it?
2. How can I avoid the "accountability spiral"?
3. Should I ask questions when I already have the answer?
4. Why shouldn't I try to solve everyone's problems?
5. If I'm busy and a coworker asks me a question, what should I do?
6. In a crisis, is it better to ask or command?
7. When should I pick up a shovel and pitch in?
8. Do you *think,* or do you *know*?

Clarity

1. How can I avoid getting "wishy-washy" answers?
2. How does dissonance point to problems and opportunities?
3. How can I identify fallacious arguments?
4. Are there really no stupid questions?
5. How can I seek clarification without being judgmental?
6. How did curiosity kill the leader?
7. When is no answer the best answer?
8. When should I seek complex solutions to problems?

9. What question didn't I ask?
10. When should I go over a coworker's head to achieve my goals?
11. When should I provide solutions for my team?
12. How can I keep meetings on track?

Objectivity

1. What causes people to shut down and disengage from conversation?
2. What did I miss when I *Blink*ed?
3. What should I do if I encounter conflicting data?
4. We've always done it that way, but *why*?
5. Why is it important to make a distinction between me, the leader, and me, the person?

Create Better Decisions (Context) #1:
Whose decision is it?

As clients meet with me to discuss leadership, inevitably the conversation turns to decision making. Making decisions is one of the most taxing job responsibilities for leaders. In my experience, leaders suffer more than they should because they make too many decisions. Often, it's because they fail to ask, "Whose decision is it?"

When leaders take the burden of responsibility too far, they either want to protect others from making tough decisions or they want to extend their power. The result is poor decision making because these leaders don't have sufficient information. To make matters worse, the coworkers who should make these decisions don't gain valuable experience. Instead of adhering to the old Harry S. Truman adage "the buck stops here," these leaders should do a better job of clarifying job responsibilities, trusting their coworkers to make good decisions, and then holding them accountable.

Lord Carrington, whom I knew for a brief time, was minister of the British Defense Department during the Falkland Islands war. The war was launched because of a mistake a British radio operator made on one of the frigates out at sea. Lord Carrington was obligated via ministerial responsibility (the British version of "the buck stops here") to resign. After all, if he was doing his job, all those under his command must be doing their jobs, too, no matter how far removed—including the radio operator. This practice is outdated, in part, because it takes accountability away from the person who is directly responsible. And it results in leaders who are either too controlling or unjustly blamed for the bad decisions of others.

"Perhaps you can help me with a problem I'm having," Todd said as we sat down for coffee. Todd is a dear friend who runs one of the largest financial services companies on the East Coast. "I have this woman who works for me. She's grown her department by 30 percent in the last year, but she hasn't been showing up at the weekly executive meetings even when she's in the office. Her boss thinks everything's fine and keeps citing the 30 percent figure, but the competition in that industry segment is scoring even higher. Plus, her department is the doorway into my company for many customers." I asked Todd what exactly the problem was. He said, "Her!"

"Are you sure?" I asked.

Todd looked at me quizzically. I asked him whom she reported to. He said, "She reports to Dave." I then asked, "So whose problem is it?" Begrudgingly, he said, "Dave's."

As a leader, Todd shouldn't ignore the fact that he had heard complaints about this particular employee. Instead, he must hold Dave accountable for his people. Once Dave is alerted to the issue, it's no longer Todd's issue. If Dave fails to correct the problem, however, then Todd must confront a new issue: Dave's failure to manage his charges.

Because the failure of the employee to attend his meeting affects Todd, I suggested a strategy that helps set clear boundaries. I encouraged him to cancel the next meeting if one or more people didn't attend. The message would be loud and clear: everyone's participation is critical to the process. And, based upon my experience, I doubt Todd would have to cancel more than one meeting.

Employee empowerment begins with leaders asking themselves four words over and over: "Whose decision is it?" Because coworkers might assume that leaders are exempt from the rules and can make any and all decisions, leaders must be extra vigilant about asking this question.

Create Better Decisions (Context) #2:

How can I avoid the "accountability spiral"?

As part of a close-knit leadership team, you may be reluctant to ask tough questions of one another. A lot rides on maintaining friendly bonds with your fellow leaders. But when leaders don't ask tough questions of one another, accountability tends to spiral downward— toward lower-level workers who aren't present.

Take this scenario: "We're behind on our numbers because of Larry *again*. He does good work, but deadlines for him are never final. If I want a report on my desk by Friday afternoon, he thinks that means first thing Monday morning!" While Larry's procrastination may be the source of the problem, his manager's failure is a bigger concern. Her job, after all, is to ensure that Larry does his.

The best way to build accountability is to start at the top. If all team leaders are held accountable for the performance of their units, they will employ strategies that ensure that their coworkers achieve success. Larry will know that his procrastination isn't his issue alone. His work isn't just a reflection of his manager; it is, in effect, her work, too. And if he doesn't learn that, then his time in the organization will be short lived.

Don't let accountability spiral downward. Hold everyone on the leadership team accountable. When a fellow leader badmouths "Larry," don't cluck your tongue and offer sympathy. Ask, "What are you doing to solve Larry's problem?"

Create Better Decisions (Context) #3:

Should I ask questions when I already have the answer?

According to Will Lansing, CEO and chairman of ShopNBC, "I ask questions to learn things that I don't know. I want to be transparent to my people. I never ask questions I have the answers to. My time is too valuable to waste playing games with my team, and they know it."

Will learned a lot from working with Jack Welch at General Electric. He recalled when Jack's understanding of the plastics business didn't match a report made by a manager in that particular division. Jack had an engineering degree and grew up in the plastics business, but he didn't assume that he was right and the other person wrong. He began by asking how the plastics business had changed in the past five years, with the intention of updating his knowledge and perhaps reconciling the difference in opinion. "His goal was not to trap or trick his management team," said Will, "but to understand their perspective on the business that leads to their decision making."

Most leaders don't believe that question-based leadership means that their businesses must, therefore, become democracies. When consensus isn't reached, leaders must make unilateral decisions. If, however, their decisions always swing the way of their initial opinion, the quality of input from others will likely decrease over time.

Will is always prepared to reassess his position. As a result, his team feels comfortable sharing new insights, perspectives, and knowledge even after he's made a decision.

Ask questions you want to know the answer to, but don't assume that your decisions or knowledge can't be improved.

Create Better Decisions (Context) #4:

Why shouldn't I try to solve everyone's problems?

People often walk into my office with a problem. If I'm in a good place, I'll ask many questions and help them solve their problem, so they can feel good about themselves. If I'm in a bad place (low self-esteem, for example), I'll ask questions that would help me solve the problem for them, so I can feel good about myself. The nature of the questions change because the same questions that would help me solve the problem may be very different from the ones they need to hear.

When we are solving someone else's problem, we ask for all the background on the subject. After a lengthy fact-finding mission, we try to match the current problem with a solution from the secondhand bin (our memory of past successes). Unfortunately, this process rarely succeeds because *we can't possibly know as much as the person with the problem.*

If I asked you to describe yesterday to me, you would probably summarize your day in about five minutes. If you're a good storyteller, you might go off on a tangent for five more minutes. If pressed, you might be able to add another 20 minutes of detail. The likelihood of you taking an entire day to describe what you did, observed, and thought would be remote at best.

Lester Crown is a member of the Maytag Board and one of the wealthiest men in the world according to *Forbes.* As a mentor, he helped cure me of my desire to solve others' problems. He told me, "Someone who spends five days a week, eight hours a day, or the equivalent of 2,000 hours a year, is much more likely to know how to perform their job and solve their problems than I will, especially if I am doing my job, not theirs."

The person best equipped to solve a problem is the one who lives with it every day. Don't make decisions for your coworkers. With questions, help them expand their consciousness so that they can see the world anew. Help them make their own decisions.

Create Better Decisions (Context) #5:

If I'm busy and a coworker asks me a question, what should I do?

If you receive an unscheduled visit from a coworker, assess the relative urgency of your current activity and the coworker's need before making a decision.

A coworker says, "I just have a quick question for you before you leave." You're slipping your coat over one arm, juggling your briefcase in the other. Against your better judgment, you say, "How can I help?" You've put up a yield sign and the coworker races through it: "Do you think I should run this ad next week?"

While half your brain is focusing on your scheduled activity, you're also thinking: "Is this something I should be deciding? Do I want to make this decision without further discussion or input from others? When does this decision need to be made? What if I say no?" Instead of voicing these concerns, you say, "Yes" and keep on walking out the door.

The following week, you realize the cost of that snap decision. Because the direct mail campaign launched late and the 1–800 number on the ad didn't get directed to the call center, you're putting out fires all week—all because you didn't provide time for proper deliberation and questioning.

Imagine what would have happened if you had simply asked about the urgency of the decision: "When does this decision need to be made?" If your coworker said, "By tomorrow afternoon," you could delay the decision until you had more time and information. "Great," you might have said, "why don't you get on my calendar for half an hour between now and then, and make sure you come with your recommendation?"

In the future, by quickly identifying the level of urgency, you'll avoid making decisions that are not really yours to make. Often it's not a coincidence that coworkers ask important questions just as you're on your way out. They may want you to take or share responsibility for decisions they themselves ought to make. If a coworker does this regularly, recognize it for what it is: responsibility avoidance. And take steps to curb this behavior pattern.

What if the coworker said that the decision needed to be made in the next hour? If time is of the essence, determine the decision's significance. You might ask, "What are the consequences of making the wrong decision?"

Once you learned about the potential breach between the call center and the direct mailers, you would weigh it against your previously scheduled activity and its relative urgency. Even if you were meeting your boss or a peer for lunch, you ought not to think twice about canceling. No commitment, unless it takes a higher priority to help you achieve the company's overall goal, should keep you from assisting with your coworker's dilemma. Leadership is about allocation of resources, and you are one of the company's most valuable resources. Once the situation has been dealt with, however, address the coworker's failure to bring this decision to your attention earlier.

If you get caught in the hall or on your way out, do a quick calculation involving your scheduled activity, your coworker's need, and the relative urgency of both. Ask questions that establish the timeframe and significance of your coworker's need, so you can make an informed decision.

Create Better Decisions (Context) #6:

In a crisis, is it better to ask or command?

The conventional wisdom would have you believe that when the pressure is on, leaders should tighten up the reins, ask less, and tell more. Research done by the National Aeronautics and Space Administration (NASA) suggests otherwise.

In an article titled "Effective Crisis Management" (*New Management*, Summer 1985), Robert Blake and Jane Mouton from NASA's Ames Research Center, who investigated aviation failures in the 1970s, said, "The pilots learned that when a captain centralizes authority in himself, he in effect shuts out information that others are capable of contributing. The pilots learned from experience that they were failing to recognize that others have knowledge and may be able to contribute to a valid and safe resolution of a crisis."

The British learned a similar lesson when German U-boats were sinking merchant ships in World War II. When the ships were hit and the crews disembarked, it was not the younger, more fit merchant marines who survived; it was the older ones. Kurt Hahn, a leading educator at the time, discovered that older seamen were more inclined to listen to others and work out a survival plan together—despite the imminent dangers. Interestingly, from this research, Outward Bound was born.

If pilots (facing the likelihood of a crash) and merchant marines (aboard a torpedoed ship) can make time to ask questions and consider alternatives, then perhaps you have the time to listen to what your coworkers have to say, even under duress.

123

Create Better Decisions (Context) #7:

When should I pick up a shovel and pitch in?

Leaders want to be good role models for their coworkers, so sometimes they put on a hard hat or lick envelopes to demonstrate that they're not above anyone or any job in the organization. While the impulse is noble, it's a bad idea.

The data department in your organization is up all night dealing with an issue that will drastically affect quarterly earnings. To be a good role model, you stay up all night. While you might be doing some short-term good (reducing everyone's workload by a fraction), there are long-term consequences. You send your coworkers the message that you don't trust them. And, frankly, they might not appreciate the added tension of having to work side by side with you when there's already plenty of incentive to get the job done. They might wonder, "Don't you have more important things to do?" or "How is your energy going to be the next day when you're needed to lead through this crisis?"

In trying to be the hero, you are likely doing more harm than good. First of all, your coworkers may have to spend some of their valuable time teaching you how to do their jobs. And, if you do their jobs easily and well, it might very well lower their morale, if they take pride in what they do. No short-term fix is worth lowering morale—something that's very hard to build.

Leaders need to be the visionary, the strategist—not the frontline worker. Rather than picking up a shovel, pick up the phone. Make sure your coworkers have the resources and personnel they need, so that all-nighters are an aberration, not something they come to resent.

Create Better Decisions (Context) #8: Do you *think,* or do you *know*?

All living things are changing or decomposing, so we can't have exact knowledge of them. According to Plato, only reason is eternally and universally precise.

Try asking your coworkers, "Do you *think,* or do you *know?*" It's a question that can help determine if they are coming to you with theories and feelings or with knowledge gained from thorough reasoning and research. I got this valuable question from Chris Mahai, a partner at Aveus, who got it from one of her clients.

Like Plato, Heraclitus believed in the ever-changing nature of the world. He said, "We cannot step twice into the same river." As a cofounder of ACI, I did most jobs in the company at one time or another. About 14 years into the business, we were having strategic discussions about sales, and I volunteered a solution. Lois Dirksen, the executive vice president of sales and service at ACI, said, "Gary, we now have 100-page scripts, not three pages, and the size of the database is a hundred times what it was." Needless to say, the process (or "river") had changed. I should have been asking questions and acquiring wisdom instead of assuming I still knew the answers.

Socrates loved wisdom, but didn't consider himself to be a sophist. The more he learned, the more he realized how much more there was to learn. Questions were critical to his learning process. He always sought definitions early on in the discussion. If, for instance, the topic was "What is great leadership?" he would ask for a definition of *leadership.* Just the act of defining terms accelerated and clarified thinking.

Disputes and disagreements often occur because a topic is defined differently by both parties. Make sure you and your coworkers are working with the same definition. Starting on common ground is important, but so is getting accurate results—knowledge, in other words. Don't be satisfied with what your coworkers think or feel. Make them demonstrate their positions with reason and research.

Create Better Decisions (Clarity) #1:

How can I avoid getting "wishy-washy" answers?

On the TV sitcom *Seinfeld*, if customers at a popular takeout restaurant hemmed and hawed about their order, the man taking the orders, the "Soup Nazi," would shout, "No soup for you!" I know the COO of a high-tech company who takes a similar approach. If his coworkers don't come up with quick, accurate answers to his questions, he will instruct them not to return to his office until they do.

Are you tired of hearing "about," "perhaps," "maybe," "possible," "a lot," and "a little"? Wouldn't you rather hear, "I will complete this task by noon on the 27th," "We have 20 closed accounts as of 8 a.m. this morning," and "Revenue will be short by $200,024 this month unless account ABC closes by the end of business today"?

Don't accept "wishy-washy" answers. Don't let lazy or unprepared coworkers off the hook. Keep the questions coming.

Some leaders follow the "Five Why" rule. They don't stop asking, "Why?" until they have asked it five times in a row. Granted, this can be annoying, especially for those who have young children. But once your coworkers have been conditioned to expect, "Why?" your need to ask it will diminish over time. Instead your questions will start to be more exploratory and forward-looking (e.g., "How might we apply this information to other business practices?") and less focused on meeting deadlines and keeping coworkers on task.

The former secretary of defense, Donald Rumsfeld, used to send out memos to his staff in a flurry. These memos, known as "snowflakes" in the Pentagon, might have been as simple as an FYI ("for your information") about a certain topic. When the secretary of defense sends you an FYI, there is still a question attached to it: "Did you know about this?" If not, then you should get up to speed. In some of his other memos, the questions were not veiled. "What do you know about this?" might have appeared with a request for a response by a specified date.

Ask, "Why?" and follow up on the FYIs or "snowflakes" that you send. When you slow down the rate of questions, the answers slow down, too.

Create Better Decisions (Clarity) #2:

How does dissonance point to problems and opportunities?

Dissonance is a combination of sounds that are discordant and unstable—in conflict, in other words. Thomas Urban, former CEO and chairman of Pioneer Hi-Bred International, looked for conflict between what his coworkers said and how they acted. If a coworker spoke enthusiastically about a project but failed to make eye contact, for instance, Tom's dissonance detector went off.

If you're hearing one thing but seeing or sensing another, plumb the dissonance. If there's a gap between the work done and the work you expected to be done, study your coworkers' body language. Try to pick up on nonverbal cues being transmitted. Are their voices lowered or trailing off? Do they look uncomfortable? Are they leaning toward the door?

When Tom detected dissonance, he tried to imagine the question the speaker least wanted him to ask. Then he asked it. Interestingly, Tom found it easier to listen for dissonance and ask the right questions if the organization's vision, plan, and goals were clear. After all, if he knew what key the symphony was in, it was much easier to detect a wrong note.

Of course, you should be as attuned to your own body language as you are to your coworkers'. Maintain eye contact. Sit up straight and lean forward. Don't communicate disinterest or impatience by tapping a pen against the desk. Make sure your mouth and body are sending the same message.

Create Better Decisions (Clarity) #3:
How can I identify fallacious arguments?

A fallacy is a misconception resulting from incorrect reasoning—the result, often, of deceptive behavior. Learn to recognize fallacious arguments and you will start seeing new solutions, know when to ask for clarification, and avoid being manipulated.

Loaded questions are perhaps the easiest fallacious arguments to detect. They don't allow responders a viable exit. I might, for example, ask my eldest daughter, "Are you still beating up your sister?" If she answers, "No!" she admits to beating up her sister earlier. If she answers, "Yes!" she also admits wrongdoing. Since this is an established joke in our family, the consequences aren't significant. Imagine, though, if a boss asks his employee, "Are you still having an issue with that software?" when, in fact, the employee isn't having problems and never has. Unless the employee has the presence of mind to expose the question's unfairness, she looks bad. Worse, she might assume that one of her coworkers reported these alleged struggles to the boss—creating a culture of distrust. In all likelihood, she would simply answer, "No," and then commence an investigation of her colleagues, replay her own recent and past interactions with the boss, and seek an assessment of her software abilities—a waste of her time, at the very least.

Intentional ambiguity is another type of fallacious argument. Consider President Clinton's statement about his relationship with Monica Lewinsky: "I did not have sexual relations with that woman." By "sexual relations," Clinton meant that he had not had sexual intercourse with Lewinsky. He took a narrow view of the term but hoped that others would accept the broader implications of the term (meaning that he had no sexual contact with her at all). Of course, this intentional ambiguity was eventually exposed and contributed to his impeachment.

Guilt-by-association fallacies stem from ill-formed logic and laziness. Here's an example: "If company XYZ has displayed some unethical behavior in the past, then all their new practices must be unethical, too." Such statements must be exploded with questions that illustrate the dangers of simple-minded, reductive habits. Ask, "Can you think of one case when they behaved ethically?" or, "Has our organization ever made an ethical breach?" and "Haven't we taken steps to prevent that from happening again in the future?" Otherwise, you might not learn about practices or products that might prove valuable to your organization.

Fallacious arguments are often "outs" for people who feel stumped or frustrated in the face of superior or antithetical logic. Mark Kennedy, a congressman from Minnesota, couldn't convince me that more nuclear weapons would improve the safety of the United States.

Rather than continue his line of reasoning, he asked, "Do you want nuclear armament or a national security risk?" I recognized the loaded question and answered, "Do you think of this issue that simply?"

Recognize fallacious arguments for what they are: traps. A terrific list of such arguments appears on Don Lindsay's Web site (http://www.don-lindsay-archive.org/skeptic/arguments.html) and fallacyfiles.org (where I found the Monica Lewinski example above). The more versed you are in fallacious arguments, the better prepared you will be to ask questions that will improve and clarify the thinking of your coworkers.

Create Better Decisions (Clarity) #4:

Are there really no stupid questions?

"There are no stupid questions," says Steve Wolff, CEO of AMS, a consulting company for the performing arts. In fact, questions that begin, "This may be a stupid question, but ..." are devilishly effective. They can not only prevent misunderstandings but also keep expectations in check.

As a consultant, Steve is paid to ask questions. He's found that asking "stupid" questions gets people to open up, whereas pointed questions can put people on the defensive (at least initially). When Steve spoke with the board of a new art theater, he asked, "This may be a stupid question, but why are you building this theater?"

The chair of the committee responded, "Not at all. Great question." When in the midst of a huge project, people can get so focused on *how* it will be accomplished, they often neglect the *why*. This might explain why the members of the committee proceeded to have a long, productive conversation about their vision for the theater. Steve learned that some committee members believed that this community theater would immediately be the next Kennedy Center. Steve asked more "stupid" questions that guided them to more realistic expectations. After all, the Kennedy Center, in Washington, D.C., was built in the 1960s and has spent decades building a loyal following.

Columbo, the TV detective, mastered the art of looking confused when interrogating a suspect. Columbo's suspects were, of course, actors working from a script. So beware. If you dumb it down too much, your coworkers or clients won't confide in you. They might even wonder how you got your leadership position. But, if your questions are open-ended and your questions become less "stupid" as they expose misunderstanding or unrealistic expectations, your results will rival Columbo's.

Yale Dolginow, president and CEO of Paper Warehouse, is another "stupid question" proselytizer. At the second meeting of a bank board, his head was awash with acronyms. He asked, "This might be a stupid question, but do you have a sheet that defines all these acronyms?" The board member next to him said, "That's a great idea. I still don't know what half of them mean." He'd been on the board for 11 years!

Don't let shame or embarrassment prevent you from admitting what you don't know. Consider it an opportunity to revisit protocols or decisions. What "stupid questions" have you been holding back?

Create Better Decisions (Clarity) #5:

How can I seek clarification without being judgmental?

When judgment sneaks into questions, you would be better off not asking anything at all. Judgment-laden questions like "You decided to send the survey to our customers even though you knew it was full of misspellings?" are a passive aggressive way to express your own opinion and diminish others. They provoke defensive "fight or flight" reactions and serve as a deterrent to initiative and risk taking (See "Are my values in alignment with the four core human drives?" in Chapter 1 and "What causes people to shut down and disengage from conversation?" later in this chapter).

We would all do well to take a page from the Quakers. A clearness committee convenes when a member of the Quaker community needs help. The group's sole purpose is to give the troubled member clarity. First, the person who called the meeting describes the situation. The group then acts without providing judgment, opinions, or insights. They operate on the assumption that the

133

person has the capacity to resolve the situation. As a precaution, joiner questions or follow-up questions are prohibited, since they would likely nudge the one in need toward a particular decision. Each question must stand independently.

A dear friend of mine asked a close circle of friends to assist him with a personal problem, in the tradition of the Quaker clearness committee. He's a psychologist, and when a member of the committee asked, "If you were your own client, what would you do?" the answer came to my friend instantly. Two years later, he still talks about how good it felt to resolve the issue "on his own."

In my coaching business, when clients tell me a story, I often ask them to pause after the line, "I told him/her/them to . . . "

"If you had asked a question, what would it be?" I ask.

If they act on impulse, they will typically shift to a judgment question—only marginally better (and sometimes worse) than, "I told them to . . . "

"How would that question be helpful?"

The response invariably is, "It wouldn't."

"What question could you ask without judgment?"

It can take a while to come up with a solution to this question. That's because judgment questions are simple, easy to form ("Why did you do *that*?"), and ego-boosting.

To break from the mental pattern of judgment questions takes hard work. Good questions must be authentic, not leading. You must have a genuine interest in the answer. And you have to be willing to cede the discovery of the solution to your coworker(s).

Are your questions laced with judgment? Do you already have an opinion formed before your question is asked? If so, you're not putting yourself in a position to help your coworkers. You should turn the critical lens inward. Ask, "Why do I need to be the one who is always right? Why do I always need to get credit for the solution?"

Create Better Decisions (Clarity) #6:
How did curiosity kill the leader?

When you log onto the Internet, do you stay focused on your search, or do you occasionally follow strings of curiosity? If you're like most leaders, you're curious. You ask "Why?" questions a lot. These questions and your curiosity often lead to innovative solutions. On the other hand, problems can arise when your curiosity takes someone else for a ride.

If you're conversing with coworkers about their work, be sure to frame your questions. Explain why you're asking a particular question (you want to gather information to make a decision yourself *or* you want to learn about how this person is making a particular decision, for example), so that your coworkers don't make assumptions about what they should or shouldn't be

135

doing. If you fail to frame your questions, even if the setting is informal, your coworkers might assume that you want them to set a new course using your questions as a guide. They might, for instance, take a simple clarification question (e.g., "Why are you using the hand-carved ornaments?") as an indication that they should have made a different decision (e.g., factory-made ornaments).

Tom Urban wandered around Pioneer Hi-Bred International at least one day each month. He would walk into someone's cube, look at the nameplate, and ask a specific question. "So, Carol," he might begin, "any new surprises in accounting lately?" Whether there happened to be any new surprises or not, Tom always shared the reason for his question before leaving ("I wanted to know how we managed to reduce legal costs this quarter."). He found if he didn't communicate the "why," the coworker was likely to wonder about the reason for the CEO's visit. Carol, for instance, might have wondered, *Was there an accounting surprise that I should have found? Maybe I should reexamine my process.*

The old adage "a small turn from the captain of the ship will turn major wheels down below" holds true. Know clearly what you want to accomplish with your questions and frame your questions so your coworkers know the "why." If you aren't clear, you might wind up with unintended consequences—like factory-made ornaments or an unnecessary shift in accounting practices.

Create Better Decisions (Clarity) #7:
When is no answer the best answer?

"Be helpless, dumbfounded, unable to say yes or no." This line from Rumi's poem, "Zero Circle" suggests that it's okay to put off a decision.

As leaders, we're expected to have answers. A quick answer, though, is not always the right answer. It's best to give silence and thought to questions. In the process you'll open yourself up to possibilities.

When others feel discomfort because they can't solve a problem, we want to help. We absorb some of their discomfort, creating even more pressure for a quick answer. Pausing and considering the question from all angles can feel like needless delay. But sitting in that "helpless" liminal space can provide valuable insights. You might determine, for example, that the true nature of the problem is hiding behind a faulty question.

As ACI Telecentrics grew, Rick and I were eager to provide call center services to Fortune 500 businesses, since they would provide us with two to five million dollars in annual revenue. We found, however, that although we were allowed to participate in the request-for-proposal (RFP) process, we didn't get site visits. At executive team meetings we repeatedly asked ourselves, "How can we win our prospects' business?" Only after we sat on this question for a long time did we realize the question we should have been asking: "How can we win the RFP process?"

137

The first question was so large, it was impossible to take action on it. In asking the more manageable RFP question, it occurred to us that our clients might have the answer. We asked them why they bought our services, but found no commonality in their responses. Then we asked a client if he would send us all of our competitors' proposals. He agreed, and we spent countless hours sifting through stacks of 60-page reports. Because some of our competitors were billion-dollar enterprises, we couldn't offer all that they could, but we could hire a writer to make our reports better than most. So we did. We began winning three out of four RFPs and received site visits, which pushed us one step further along in the sales process.

Not everyone can sit in limbo, waiting for the right question or answer to reveal itself. When I feel stuck, I often reach for food. Others reach for cigarettes. Some reach for their to-do list to stay busy. Some reach for chemicals. You may call peers, mentors, or family to help you get your bearings, and yet often all that is needed is stillness. Set down the phone, turn off the BlackBerry, and ignore the tidal wave of incoming information. Sit still.

I once heard David Whyte recite a poem by David Wagoner called "Lost." The poem addresses the question of what to do when you're lost in the woods. Rather than run off in any direction, hoping it's the right one, the poem suggests you "stand still. The forest knows where you are. You must let it find you." Learn the forest—tree by tree, gurgling brook by gurgling brook, mossy stone by mossy stone—before you act, so that you don't run in circles.

Don't let anxiety guide you. Take time to familiarize yourself fully with the problem before settling on an answer.

Create Better Decisions (Clarity) #8:

When should I seek complex solutions to problems?

The best litmus test for whether a problem is simple or complex comes from the book *Making Things Happen* by Scott Berkun (O'Reilly Media, Inc., 2008). If the problem takes a long time to describe, it's complex. If not, it's simple.

For simple problems, chances are you can find the root cause easily and derive a solution. For complex problems, the root cause is often hard to identify and just as hard, if not harder, to solve. In my experience, complex problems are usually best resolved by moving the decision making down to the level that is experiencing the problem. Consequently, knowing the nature of the problem (simple or complicated) can prevent you from trying a quick solution that only will be attending to a symptom of the underlying problem.

Tom Pritzker, chairman of Hyatt Corporation and Marmon Group Holdings, shared with me a story about how one complex workplace problem was solved. One of the companies he's invested in had an opportunity to take on a big order from the military. The CEO asked the plant manager if he could cut the assembly time from six-and-a-half hours to four to accommodate the new order. The plant manager said the plant was at capacity and wouldn't be able to produce the order in the timeline required; he had engineered the line himself and assured the CEO that it didn't have any more throughput.

Rather than give up, the CEO decided to put the question to the assembly team. They shut down the line and in came these guys with rolled-up t-shirts, clean-shaven heads, and huge biceps. The first assembly line worker said, "I don't know how we can speed up the entire line, but I could shave considerable time from my area if I could get shelves installed to stock inventory by my machine." After all the workers were given a chance to show how they might accelerate the process, they had cut the production time down not to four hours but to three! As a result, not only did the CEO take the big new order but the company also saw a huge reduction in labor cost per item for all its business.

Sometimes even simple problems benefit from complex solutions. At the Science Museum in St. Paul, Minnesota, I watched as two fourth-grade classes from my daughter's school matched up with their pen pals from another school. One teacher took students individually and paired them with their pen pals, since they had never met in person before. Another teacher asked students just to go and find their buddies. Which solution do you think worked faster for this coordination problem? The latter. Allowing those closest to the problem solve it proved to be twice as fast as the command-and-control approach.

Later in the day, there was another opportunity to test these two approaches. The teachers needed to ensure that all students were present and accounted for before they left the museum. One teacher took his class list and checked off students as he spotted them. The other teacher asked her class to count off from 1 to 20 (the numbers had been previously assigned to the kids). With their consent, I timed the two teachers using a stopwatch. The count-off process won, hands down. Again, the complex solution (requiring the involvement of many students) proved much faster than the simple solution.

Before you go on the hunt for a solution by yourself, ask, "Is the problem complex or simple?" If it's complex, take the problem to its source; move it down the organization. Complex problems require complex solutions. Sometimes even simple problems benefit from complex solutions, so be open to new methods. In general, trust those who are most familiar with the problem to make the right decisions.

Create Better Decisions (Clarity) #9:
What question didn't I ask?

A CEO friend turned her retail company around by closing nonproductive assets, cutting costs, and retooling merchandise over the course of a year. While shareholders saw a significant return, her compensation did not rise similarly. So, prior to the next board meeting, this CEO made her case for a raise to each board member individually—"Just like the textbook says to do," she said.

The work of supervisory boards is rarely completed in the boardroom. Meetings are often just a place to rubber-stamp decisions that have been hashed out beforehand. So imagine this CEO's surprise when she learned that the board voted down the increased compensation—after every single board member had agreed to support her cause privately.

It turned out that one of the board members was being investigated by the Securities and Exchange Commission (SEC) for his role in another company's dealings. He didn't want to give the SEC the tiniest hint of impropriety. Increasing compensation, he felt, might draw the SEC's attention. His passion and/or paranoia were so convincing that the other board members were eventually swayed.

Reflecting later, the CEO realized that there was one question she failed to ask of everyone: "What is the one thing that would prevent you from voting for this?" If she had asked this, she believes she could have achieved a different outcome.

What is the one question you haven't asked? Be sure to ask it before a decision is made.

Create Better Decisions (Clarity) #10:

When should I go over a coworker's head to achieve my goals?

Before becoming CEO of EZ Payroll & Staffing, Kayle Neeley was a vice president for Norwegian Cruise Line, one of the world's largest travel companies. He was recruited to do for them what he had done for three other organizations in the past: install a unique marketing system that increases revenue dramatically. Despite his impressive track record, starting up a new business unit within a monolithic company presented considerable challenges. Kayle had to dance with the elephants and swim with the sharks to get his goals met—while constantly bumping up against bureaucracy and fiefdoms.

143

When Kayle told his boss, subordinates, or peers what he wanted or needed from them in order to achieve his goals, he often met resistance. I asked him, "What if you asked them a question instead?" He wondered, "What would that question be?" This is where true leaders roll up their sleeves and earn their money. We discussed the nuances of the problems for 10 to 20 minutes (e.g., the people involved, roles, company mission, situation specifics) until he came to clarity about what the right question would be. I then asked him to imagine the reaction of those involved. Kayle paused and said, "They would have gone along with it without a fight. I wouldn't have had to explain my position over and over and demonstrate how this would best serve the company."

Kayle once presented a detailed plan of how the payment system was going to bill the consumer for the travel program. He estimated that the annual revenue for this program would be in the hundreds of millions of dollars; it was critical to the overall success of the business. When the accounting department saw the plan, its reaction was "I'm sorry, but you'll have to delay the plans for this project. We'll need to add too many staff to our department to deal with the increase in volume because our new billing system isn't online yet." Kayle was boiling inside when he got this message. Picture Popeye with steam whistling out of his ears and corncob pipe.

My friend was ready to hit the hallways of "mahogany row" to make his case with the chairman of financial operations (CFO) and CEO. He started imagining what he was going to say. He'd done this before and eventually won the day, but not without a strong emotional cost and some lost relationships. Nobody likes to lose a battle, even if (sometimes *especially if*) they're on the same team.

This time, however, Kayle paused and recalled my motto: Just Ask. Instead of putting together a Power-Point show, demonstrating the cost delays to this revenue stream and making a case for its importance to the corporation, he simply wrote a short e-mail to the accounting department. It read, "How many more staff will you need to add?" Its response: "Only two additional employees." End of conflict. The CFO would never bring up such a paltry inconvenience to the CEO with such a significant revenue stream at stake. My friend learned that asking questions not only helps motivate employees but also can prevent intracompany battles.

Don't go over a coworker's head without first seeking clarity by asking questions.

Create Better Decisions (Clarity) #11:
When should I provide solutions for my team?

A friend of mine, who has worked primarily at large Fortune 500 companies, assumes that by the time her coworkers come to her, they have exhausted all possible solutions. She believes that strongly in their capability.

When I asked her whether, in hindsight, she found this to be true—did her coworkers actually do all the hard work of seeking the best solution, she answered, "No." Because her coworkers know that occasionally she'll do the heavy lifting to solve a problem, they don't always push themselves to find answers. She strives to be a Teflon Woman—keeping problems from sticking to her. Now she's trying even harder. To be an effective leader, she knows that she has to be more resolute in delegating responsibility and creating authority. She must hold coworkers accountable for their own areas of responsibility.

When coworkers come in to see her, she now asks, "What have you done to deal with this problem? Where else might you go to solve this issue?" They turn and walk out the door, knowing that she won't be doing their work. Some coworkers adjust to this framework sooner and easier than others. By maintaining the questioning posture, though, she can better assess whether they have truly exhausted all possible solutions within their grasp.

Leaders who fall into the trap of completing their team's work not only are stifling their coworkers' growth, they also are holding back their organization's growth. If the leader is called upon to solve all or most problems, the organization does not benefit from the brainpower of all of its employees. If the leader leaves or is unavailable, the remaining employees won't be equipped to solve problems on their own. On the other hand, if the leader asks his or her team members to solve problems they encounter, there is a possibility for new and innovative thinking. And individuals will be motivated to be part of the solution rather than part of the problem.

Assumptions like "when my team comes to me for help they must have exhausted all possible solutions" are hard to shake. Organizational assumptions can become chronic. In one organization I observed, the outgoing leader didn't want salespeople to work remotely. This assumption became so ingrained that when leadership changed, the rule about not working remotely remained. Some highly qualified sales job candidates were not hired as a result. When the new leader questioned this process, he was told, "It's always been that way."

Leaders must continually question assumptions—their own and others'. Often vice presidents are not willing to question everything, so this becomes even a larger task for the president or CEO to accomplish. The exceptional leaders I know challenge assumptions with questions. In the process, members of their teams become dynamic and innovative leaders in their own right.

Create Better Decisions (Clarity) #12:
How can I keep meetings on track?

Bob Aronson is one of the most respected communication consultants in the country. He believes in question-based leadership, but he uses one question more than all others: "So what?"

Bob got tired of meetings running on interminably because of irrelevant or uninspired comments. Now, any time he feels conversation veering off on one of these detours, he trots out his trademark question: "So what?"

The result: his coworkers either get to the point or they take a seat.

One of Bob's clients loved this question so much, he had it printed on everything. When you walked into any of his conference rooms blazoned on the wall, poster-size, were the words "So what?" Soon afterward, the time spent in meetings was sliced in half. The focus of the meetings became clearer. People reported feeling more productive and engaged. They no longer felt like their time was being wasted.

Give it a try and ask, "So what?" You really have nothing to lose—except half the time you spend in meetings.

Create Better Decisions (Objectivity) #1:

What causes people to shut down and disengage from conversation?

Due to the power differential between you and your coworkers, you must learn not only how to tolerate criticism but also how to restrict your criticism of others. When we're criticized, we feel like our bodies are under attack. According to neuroscientists, this fear or panic causes our prehistoric, reptilian brain to flood with blood. Rational thought is restricted, and, instead, we concentrate on our bodily impulses: fight or flight. A "flooded" person (whether it's you or a coworker) is of little use when there's a problem to be solved.

Debra, a COO of a very large food manufacturer in the Southwest, grew tired of notifying department heads about problems she found, like the shortened shelf life of a potato that was roasted in a new type of oil. "I want to know what we're doing to solve this problem!" she would demand at the beginning of a meeting. "And why didn't anyone bring this problem to my attention?" She ranted and railed because she wanted her coworkers to detect and solve these problems in the future. Unfortunately, all they heard was: "She is out to find someone to blame!" Their brains subsequently flooded, and they shifted into defense mode.

I invited Debra to consider a question-based approach to generate behavioral change. Rather than calling out individuals in a public setting (which creates more tension and, therefore, quicker flooding), here's what I suggested she do:

1. Speak with individual department heads when you detect a problem in their specific areas.

2. Start by asking a general question ("How are things going in your area?").

3. Keep an open mind. If you let the coworker dictate the conversation, you might learn that there are problems that dwarf the potato shelf life issue. Or you might find that the shelf life was a concession made as part of a larger cost/benefit calculation. Or you might find that the coworker has been having personal problems that could be contributing to poor performance.

4. If you feel like the coworker is holding back information, ask a slightly more specific question ("What are the top five priorities in your department right now?"). You might learn that the problem with the shelf life has already been detected. If so, you would now know who detected the problem, how, and when. With this information, you could set about correcting this systemic problem.

5. If the coworker does not consider the shelf life issue the top priority, ask why. You might find that you need to reorder your priorities as a result.

6. If the coworker's answer still does not take into account all the consequences you foresee, drill down one level deeper with your questions ("What impact will the shorter shelf life have on inventory?").

Even constructive criticism can feel like an attack. By asking respectful and open-ended questions, you disarm the reptilian-brain functions. No longer will coworkers be paralyzed by fight-or-flight responses. They will be prepared to work with you to detect and solve problems.

Remember that you are after the truth, not a body to hoist on a stick.

Create Better Decisions (Objectivity) #2:

What did I miss when I *Blink*ed?

In his bestselling book, *Blink: The Power of Thinking Without Thinking* (Little, Brown and Company, 2005), Malcolm Gladwell describes how intuition or snap judgments can prove superior to more analytical approaches. *Think! Why Crucial Decisions Can't Be Made in the Blink of an Eye* (Threshold Editions, 2008), a rebuttal by Michael LeGault, takes the opposite stance—espousing the importance of critical thinking.

So, whom (Gladwell or LeGault) and what (your intuition or cognitive assessment) should you follow in any given situation?

Dan Frawley, CEO of Iconoculture, advocates using both sides of your brain: the left side that manages by ordering and reasoning *and* the right side that makes more creative and associative connections. In many ways, he lets the problem dictate how much of each side he uses. If the issue is one of disorder, logic might be the best ally. If the problem is complex, intuition might provide a creative solution.

If you feel that your intuition and rational mind are in conflict, don't make a rash decision. Seek harmony between both sides of your brain. What data would confirm your intuition's impulse? What would make your rational decision *feel* better? Use questions like these to find answers that balance the equation.

151

Gen. Jack Chain was responsible for designing the B–2 Bomber. To design such a massive plane, in such a large bureaucracy as the Pentagon, takes some doing. Gen. Chain knew from his years as a pilot that there was no need for two of the plane's four seats—the ones used by navigators before the advent of navigational technology. But he needed more than intuition to convince the doubters. He asked all stakeholders, "Why are all four seats needed?" so that all conceivable defenses might surface. Once they had, he summarily dismissed them with superior logic, based largely on his knowledge of then-current technology.

It's harder, of course, to dismiss intuition than faulty logic, but intuition alone, without any logical support, does weaken eventually.

When your own intuition stubbornly resists overwhelming logic, ask yourself if you're overly swayed by one recent event or some poor historical outcomes. Since you can't turn intuition off, be sure to balance it at least with some hard questions and thorough fact finding.

Create Better Decisions (Objectivity) #3:

What should I do if I encounter conflicting data?

When faced with conflicting data, we tend to select the data that support our position and ignore the rest. That way, we can move forward quickly. *Cognitive dissonance* (the conflict of different cognitions), however, presents an opportunity to learn and improve. And we would do well to pause before making a decision.

Let's say that you let a coworker go for performance reasons. Rather than take ownership of your part in that coworker's failure, you instead focus your energy on hiring his replacement. The new hire is brimming with potential. You won't have to suffer through difficult conversations twice a week, inconsistent effort, and lapses in judgment. She will help convert the culture, manage others effortlessly, and excel on all fronts. In short, she will be able to read your mind and fulfill all your expectations.

Before you celebrate, try to reconcile the seemingly incompatible positions: yours and your former coworker's. As tempting as it might be to lay all the blame at that coworker's feet (especially since he's no longer on the premises), chances are that you contributed to his problems. In what ways could you have been more helpful and supportive? In what ways were your expectations unrealistic? What would you find frustrating about his particular job? Why might it be hard to work for you? If you don't ask and answer these questions, the shine on the new hire will dull quickly.

153

Create Better Decisions (Objectivity) #4:

"We've always done it that way," but *why*?

"We've always done it that way." These are the most irritating words uttered in organizational life. As frustrating as they are to hear, most leaders admit that they, too, have let these words escape their lips.

Mike Leary, former president of Dairy Queen Canada, actually likes to hear, "We've always done it that way." He knows this phrase implies decisions made years and years ago, and probably by people who no longer work in the organization—people who listened to eight-track tapes or rode buggies to work.

Just as seagulls are a harbinger of land, the words "we've always done it that way" are a sign of promise—the promise of more efficient and reasonable practices on the horizon.

At International Dairy Queen headquarters, Mike asked a coworker why there were five carbon copies of a particular purchasing form. The response: "We've always done it that way." "Why?" Mike asked. Thankfully, he didn't hear the dreaded, "I don't know," which would have meant more people to question, more research. Instead the coworker informed him that one form was filed alphabetically and the others were filed numerically—two downstairs and two upstairs—so that the records could be accessed easily.

Some leaders would have ended the investigation there. Mike asked, "Has anyone ever come to you and asked that you look a file up alphabetically?" He knew how the process worked, now he wanted to know *how well it worked.* "No," the coworker answered. As it turns out, the form was available and generally accessed through the corporate computer system, so all five hard copies were arguably unnecessary, not just the alphabetical one!

Here's another story from Mike's archive. In the corporate uniform department, he once overheard a customer service representative (CSR) say she did not have the authority to authorize a return of an unneeded garment. When she got off the phone, Mike asked her why she needed approval from her supervisor on such a minor matter. She responded, "We've always done it that way."

Apparently CSRs could only approve a request for the return of a garment if the request was first approved by the supervisor. Since the supervisor was frequently out of the office, CSRs had to tell customers that they had to wait, sometimes for days. Despite the frustration felt by franchise reps and CSRs, the supervisor sanctioned this convoluted process because International Dairy Queen saved money by not handling uniform returns or exchanges.

"How do you think our customers rate our CSRs' abilities when the reps are not allowed to respond to these inquiries at the time of the call?" Mike asked the supervisor. First, they discussed the consequences—both in terms of franchise/CSR/supervisor relationships and workplace atmosphere. Then Mike, the supervisor, and CSRs ironed out a policy that allowed CSRs to authorize garment requests. The result? Far less frustration and improved relationships all around.

When you hear or say, "We've always done it that way," investigate further. There's an opportunity for more efficient and reasonable practices lurking. All it takes is a little flossing. I know "flossing" sounds gross, but it might help you to remember to do it. Use questions to floss around beliefs, stories, values, and behaviors that may no longer have a place in your organization but have become embedded.

Create Better Decisions (Objectivity) #5:

Why is it important to make a distinction between me, the leader, and me, the person?

In a movie, one character may yell and even strike another character. Actors train so that their emotions and actions appear lifelike on screen. They embody their roles when the camera is rolling. Later that night, however, these same actors might go out to dinner and laugh and joke the night away. They can and must separate themselves from their roles.

The president of the United States is called "president," even by those close to him, in part to remind him that he must stay in this role (even after his term is over). He's not Barack Obama, the man; he's Barack Obama, the president of the United States. The decisions Barack Obama (the man) might make could be very different than the ones he makes as president of the United States. We, the public, might have difficulty separating Barack Obama from the role he plays, but Barack Obama must act as leader of a large and diverse country, not as a private citizen.

If you're a supervisor, manager, vice president, president, CEO, mother, father, coach, rabbi, or pastor, you're playing a leadership role. In these roles, you're either leading a part of an organization or the whole thing. The role that you play isn't who you are as a person. You will put your own personal stamp on that role, but you're not the role itself.

Ronald A. Heifetz, King Hussein bin Talal Senior Lecturer in Public Leadership at Harvard University, explained to me why this distinction is so important to make. He said that the questions you ask and the decisions you make will often be different, depending upon your role.

The other day, the woman behind the counter at the Dollar Store asked my daughter, "Do you think you should carry that much money with you?" when my daughter opened her wallet. A few days later, my daughter set her purse down at Old Navy while trying on some clothes; before she knew it, the purse was gone. An employee found it in one of the changing rooms without the money inside. You can imagine my daughter's disappointment and regret.

That evening when I called from Chicago, she shared the day's events with me. I wanted desperately to be empathetic and loving. The voice in my head was loud and clear—"Make your daughter happy, relieve her pain, and give her the money that was lost." It was not a huge amount of money to me, but it was the world to her. Instead, I listened, but I didn't take her off the emotional hook. She wasn't in imminent danger and, in the long term, she'll be better equipped to own and learn from her decisions by suffering the loss of this money. She needed her Dad at that moment, not a friend.

I've played many different roles: president, board member, follower, parent, child, and congregant. My personal reactions and beliefs don't fluctuate all that much. Only when I know and respect my roles, however, do I do justice to myself and others. Sometimes I let my private convictions be made known, but at the end of the day, I act in the best interests of those I've been charged to represent.

As an executive coach, I could benefit by asking easy questions—questions that played to the strengths of individuals or organizations. In so doing, I could get more work or even business equity. I owe it to my clients, however, to challenge them to improve their performance. I ask the difficult questions.

As a leader, be clear about your role—to yourself and others. Be aware of shifts from you, the person, to you, the leader. In almost every situation and setting, your charges will expect constancy and selflessness.

Create Better Decisions Summary

Give pause to questions. Take into account each question's urgency, your coworker's need, and the importance of your scheduled activity, before taking action. Even under extreme duress (your plane is in a tailspin or your ship is sinking), you would do well to solicit input rather than act unilaterally. The best decisions are made by those best-equipped to make them, which often means directing these decisions *down* the chain of command, not up.

If you're not happy with the quality of responses you're receiving, increase the frequency or the poignancy of your questions, or both. You will be more apt to detect dissonance and expose fallacious or lazy arguments this way. Try asking, "So what?" to encourage your coworkers to get to the point, and frame your questions, so they will better understand what your point is. When you hear "We've always done it that way," challenge the underpinnings of the assumptions in place. And when you're unsure of others' logic, don't be afraid to ask a stupid question.

Rather than succumbing to the accountability spiral, address your responsibility in the repeated failures of a coworker. Balance your intuition with logic and seek understanding, not someone to blame. Bear in mind, too, that if you don't regularly allow your opinions to be swayed, the quality of input you receive will deteriorate over time.

Leaders probe and push with a curiosity that borders on skepticism, making sure their questions are answered with action.

—JACK WELCH

CHAPTER 5

MOTIVATE TO ACTION—
ASKING FOR SUCCESS

How can you generate a sense of urgency without meeting resistance or inertia? If questions are used to intimidate, they won't inspire. Tips for building rapport, customizing incentives, and instilling respect are provided here. The goal: a safe, accepting environment that cultivates creativity and heartfelt work.

1. How do I generate a sense of urgency?
2. What would you carve your name into next to the words *made this*?
3. What leverage haven't I used?
4. How can *social proof* inspire others to follow?
5. How can shared responses energize my coworkers?

6. How do I avoid "the annoyance factor" (irritating coworkers with questions)?

7. When should I economize my questions?

8. What medium should I use—meeting, phone, or e-mail?

9. How can innuendo help me avoid confrontations?

10. How can suspending my beliefs inspire my coworkers and resolve conflicts?

11. How can feelings and identity make consensus difficult?

12. When should I use "How" and "What" questions?

13. How do I get the best out of my best performers?

14. What is the difference between challenging questions and intimidating questions?

15. Why did the Catholic Church create the devil's advocate?

16. How do I gain respect by admitting ignorance and seeking to understand?

17. Why is it so hard to hand off the leadership baton?

Motivate to Action #1:

How do I generate a sense of urgency?

According to legend, the Spanish conqueror Hernán Cortés set fire to his own ships, so that his grossly outnumbered crew would be motivated to attack the Aztecs in Mexico. With that act, he changed the question from "Why should we attack?" to "How will we win the fight?" The incentive was now eminently clear to crew members—saving their own lives. They no longer had a plan B to fall back on. Interestingly, the Aztecs, who witnessed the burning of the ships, fled in fear. They did not want any part of a fight against a foe that confident of victory.

When Janet Froetscher was hired to be executive director of United Way of Chicago, she was given the Herculean task of bringing together 54 separate United Ways in the Greater Chicago area. This had been an objective since the 1960s but had never been accomplished. Each organization stood behind its own independent and noble causes, unwilling to put aside differences and centralize power. Janet didn't set fire to any ships, but, like Cortés, she took away the escape routes for these independent organizations. She vowed to pull the charters of each United Way that didn't cooperate with the unification effort.

Once there were no escape routes for the individual United Ways, they put their attention and effort toward accomplishing the goal. Janet had changed the overarching question from "Why should we consolidate?" to "How will we consolidate?" It helped, of course, that these organizations shared a larger incentive: helping their constituents. CEOs and board members had to give up their positions, so the work was not easy, but all parties came to the table and hashed out a workable plan.

The result—the consolidation generated administrative savings of over $3 million, which fell directly to the people they served. This documented efficiency (they saved 24 cents on every dollar) in turn made it easier for United Way Chicago to generate more funding from donors far into the future.

If you cut off escape routes, all attention and effort will go to the goal. The question will change from "Why should we ...?" to "How will we ...?" The morale of your coworkers will likely be higher, though, if you have a noble goal, as Janet did, rather than threatening your crew's lives, as Cortés did!

Motivate to Action #2:

What would you carve your name into next to the words *made this*?

Former president of Dairy Queen Canada, Mike Leary, spent 30 years with International Dairy Queen, posing questions and sharing stories, as many exceptional leaders do. One of his favorite stories to tell new employees was that of a 24-year-old sculptor, Michelangelo, commissioned to create "The Pieta."

From one large slab of marble, Michelangelo carved the figure of Jesus draped over the Virgin Mary's arms and lap. The process took him nearly two years. When it was done, this masterpiece was displayed in the Chapel of Santa Petronilla, a Roman mausoleum near St. Peter's. According to legend, Michelangelo overheard someone remark that it was the work of another sculptor. That prompted Michelangelo to carve "*Michaela[n]gelus Bonarotus Florentin[us] Facieba[t]*" (Michelangelo Buonarroti, Florentine, made this) on a sash running across Mary's breasts.

When he finished this story, Mike Leary would ask his coworker, "What project or achievement here do you want to be remembered for? What would you carve your name into, next to the words *made this?*"

One of the strongest motivating factors is the desire to be remembered. Mike wanted his team to link this desire with the organization. And he wanted his team to know that their work would be appreciated with the reverence it deserved.

An important historical footnote and caution to leaders: Michelangelo always regretted his explosion of vanity and never again signed one of his works. Share this detail with your coworkers, too. Remind them that, in the end, what really matters is that you are proud to be making a meaningful contribution to the success of the organization. Due appreciation and credit will likely follow—especially if your trail of accomplishments is as impressive as Michelangelo's!

What are your coworkers sculpting that meets the needs of both the organization and the passion that they want to be known for?

165

Motivate to Action #3:

What leverage haven't I used?

Dick Seidenstricker, COO, Liberty Diversified Industries and former manager, Baxter Pharmaceutical, wondered how he could motivate his sales team at Baxter to be the best. Clearly, the trip offered to the top performers in the past wasn't enough. Or was it?

If his coworkers didn't fully appreciate a trip to Switzerland, Dick thought maybe their spouses would. Dick asked his wife to write a letter to all the other spouses saying how she had always wanted to go on one of these reward trips. She also included a brochure.

Dick received a lot of flak from his sales team, but he didn't let it deter him. Throughout the year, he sent gentle reminders to the spouses like a Swiss chocolate bar with the message, "How sweet it would be to go to Switzerland together" He also sent a Swiss Army knife with a similar message.

That year he sent three coworkers on the trip, as the sales team rose to fifth among sales regions. The following year Dick and his wife joined seven others on the trip—the result of achieving his long-sought-after goal, being the top sales region at Baxter.

When you consider the question, "How can I motivate my team?" toss out your usual bag of tricks. Try an entirely new motivational technique. Ask, "What leverage haven't I used?"

Motivate to Action #4:

How can *social proof* inspire others to follow?

We adopt the traits or preferences of people we respect and admire—a psychological tendency called *social proof*. Naturally, corporations have picked up on this tendency and employed it in their advertising.

Head was one, if not the first, sports company to hire the world's best athletes to use its products. Since many amateur skiers admired the professional athletes who used Head skis, they naturally bought Head skis for themselves. This strategy helped propel the Head brand to new heights.

Leaders have used social proof for ages to gain status or leverage. Benjamin Franklin used to roll a cart of paper down the street late in the afternoon so that customers, coworkers, and civic-oriented people saw that he was a hard worker. Because he also arrived at work early, he was in a position to question the work ethic of others: "John, getting a late start today?" he might ask.

If your coworkers admire your traits or preferences (not simply your job title), they will follow you. Bear in mind that leading, unlike skiing, is not an individual performance. The propensity of your coworkers to follow you is directly related to your ability to connect with them. Ask them about their motivations, listen to their

167

ideas, and reward them for their contributions. They, too, will become selfless askers—and inspire others in the process.

Motivate to Action #5:

How can shared responses energize my coworkers?

As new recruits pulled up to the Paris Island Marine training base, the drill sergeant screamed, "This is *my* bus, not *your* bus! Let's move, let's move, let's *move*! Do you *understand*?"

The entire group of leaders, myself included, yelled back, "Yes, sir!" We hadn't had any training. Granted, we'd probably all seen war movies, but nothing quite prepared us for the energizing feeling of yelling in unison with a group of strangers. The *esprit de corps* couldn't have been higher—and we hadn't even left the bus yet!

Tony Robbins, one of the world's best known coaches, asks his audiences to say, "Aye," if they agree. While attending Harvard Business School's Owner/President Management Program, my classmates and I went to listen to Robbins on a lark. It was free, and we thought we would have a good laugh. Instead, we walked away inspired, energetic, and enthusiastic. The event brought us closer as a group, too, simply because we'd all repeated "Aye" back to Tony in unison.

In a meeting, after you believe you have consensus, ask the group to say, "Agree." I assure you, hearing that everyone is on board will strengthen the determination of the group.

The Marines say, "Ooh-rah," and the Army says, "Hoo-ah," in response to questions. It's a way of saying, "We're all in this together and belong." How do you and your coworkers communicate this message?

Motivate to Action #6:

How do I avoid "the annoyance factor" (irritating coworkers with questions)?

Can questions become annoying? What do you think? What do you really think? Do you really think so?

Nobody likes to be barraged with questions, especially if they're all essentially the same (with slight rephrasing). People also don't like to be asked leading questions. When you receive a sour face or a particularly loud sigh, it could be because you're making coworkers fish for a specific answer. If you know exactly what you want, don't play games. This is when you should tell, not ask.

One key to avoiding the "annoyance factor" is to ask yourself, "Whose decision is it?" when coworkers first confront you with a problem. If you're the appropriate decision maker, you need to pitch your questions so that your direct reports will provide you the information you need. If not, you need to ask nonleading questions that will assist your direct reports with making their own decisions. If you're unsure about who'll make the ultimate decision, you'll often ask the wrong questions and annoy (or confuse) your coworkers.

If you're the decision maker, your first questions likely will revolve around establishing the problem. It's a mistake to try to solve problems before fully understanding their complexity. Once you have a lay of the land, brainstorm potential solutions, rank the best options, determine who'll be responsible for implementing the plan, assign a timeline and communication plan, and build in a feedback loop to ensure that all aspects have been done correctly.

Sometimes coworkers will encourage you to make a decision when, in fact, they're simply shirking their responsibility. No matter how much they slump their shoulders and give hangdog looks, you must not make their decisions for them. If you do, be prepared to make more and more decisions for them in the future. Pretty soon, you might as well assume their job titles.

How can you help others make decisions on their own? What sort of questions should you ask? How do you provide wisdom without explaining exactly how to accomplish the objective? First, be clear about your role. Here's what you might say: "I really would like to help you with this issue, but I won't provide you with an answer because this is your decision to make and I trust you to make the call." Then ask your coworkers to define the problem in detail, describe potential solutions and their relative merits, and defend the solution they currently favor. Have them jot down their own answers. Explain that you won't be doing anything with this information. The decision is still the individual coworker's to make.

If you're not the decision maker, remember that you're the teacher, not the student. If you position yourself as the student, you'll subtly suggest to your coworker that you intend to come to an independent decision about the problem (even if you never reveal your decision). By positioning yourself as the teacher, you'll impart a valuable message to your direct reports—trust. You trust them to fully establish the problem and make their own problem-solving decisions. And you've helped define boundaries—your role versus their role. Your coworkers will leave your office inspired to make good decisions.

Leaders can use questions to shirk their own responsibilities. A venture capitalist told me how the senior partners at her company provided assignments to junior associates without any explanation or resources. When the junior associates went to the seniors for help, they would engage in *annoyance factor* questioning. The junior associates would ask for direction, and the senior partners would say, "How do you think it should be done?" Inwardly the junior associates were saying, "If I knew that, I wouldn't have come to ask you!"

Sometimes leaders behave irresponsibly because they're intent on reenacting what happened to them as

171

junior associates. If I had to suffer, why should it be any different for my charges? Instead, a true leader would ask, "Why did this system work so poorly when I was a junior associate?" and, "How can we improve the performance and morale of our junior coworkers?" Leaders seek to uproot dysfunctional systems, not perpetuate them.

To avoid the *annoyance factor*, determine who is the appropriate decision maker for the problem at hand. If the decision is your coworkers' to make, let them make it. Ask nonleading questions and embody the role of teacher, not student. Be sure your coworkers have a clear objective and access to enough information and resources to complete their work. And convey your trust in them to make sound decisions.

Motivate to Action #7:

When should I economize my questions?

Gary Stern believes you can overuse, even abuse the privilege of asking questions. He says, "It's all about the economy of questions," which is fitting, coming from the head of the Federal Reserve Bank of Minneapolis.

Dieter Pape, CEO of North American Bison Cooperative, also tries to economize his questions (and avoid the *annoyance factor*). Before he and his team took the

North American Bison Cooperative out of Chapter 11 and into profitability, he grilled his vice president of sales, Tom, with questions in front of the senior team. "You have to know when to stop," Dieter said to me. "I learned from that experience. Because of all my questions, Tom became unsure of himself and felt hung out to dry in front of his peers."

If you keep firing questions at a particular coworker, she might feel inadequate and angry at you for exposing her lack of knowledge to others. Take into account the setting, the participants, and the purpose. If your coworker is in the first stage of a project, don't pepper her with questions relating to the fifth or sixth stage, unless you're certain she doesn't feel overwhelmed. Be conscious of body language and her contributions to the discussion. If they start to lag and she gets defensive or her tone drops, you've likely gone too far.

If you do go too far, you would do well to follow Dieter's lead. He apologized first to Tom in private, and then extended the apology a second time, this time in front of the entire senior team.

The public apology helped Dieter's coworkers understand both the value of questions and the damage when used inappropriately or in excess. Since then, they are more comfortable alerting Dieter to times when he's pushing the question quotient.

To his credit, Dieter is able to maintain a sense of humor about his penchant for question asking. When

173

Tom bought Dieter a large bottle of pills (jelly beans, actually) labeled "Anti-Hypothesis Pills" for his birthday, it brought down the house with laughter.

Motivate to Action #8:

What medium should I use—meeting, phone, or e-mail?

The question you ask matters, but so does the medium. Meetings enable you to detect dissonance—physical reactions or gestures that conflict with oral statements. The phone allows you to impart the proper tone. E-mail, on the other hand, doesn't interrupt the responder, is efficient, and provides a written register of the exchange.

Each medium has its share of drawbacks. Meetings take up a considerable amount of time (not just the meetings themselves, but the scheduling component) and may be impractical. The pressure to answer a call from a CEO or manager will likely cause employees to suspend whatever they are doing, maybe even leave a meeting. That's because a phone call suggests importance and the need for immediate action. E-mails can also call for immediate action, but they aren't as disruptive. On the other hand, their content may be misinterpreted, and there's no assurance when or if the recipient will read the message.

At the end of the day, e-mail is still the preferred method of communication for most people.

"I use e-mail all the time to ask questions. It's a great way to get things moving and sorted out, if you have a sense of urgency like I do," says Jerry Storch, chairman and CEO of Toys "R" Us. Recently, when dealing with a product that was unfairly deemed unsafe, Toys "R" Us pulled the product from shelves (with the intention of returning it to stores at a later date). This action prompted consumers to become more concerned about the product's safety. Jerry e-mailed five department heads, and within several hours they reached a decision. They would not continue to stock the product. "If I had done it the typical way, calling a meeting on this issue, it would have taken two weeks to get us all in the same room. Many junior executives' time would have been tied up in the meantime—putting together all the supporting data for each opinion and making them look great for the meeting. All that research would have been needed had this issue become more complicated; however, it was not that complex."

E-mail can certainly save time, if it's used appropriately. Here are several safeguards that Jerry uses to avoid the limitations of e-mail:

1. He takes pains to convince the e-mail recipient that the question he is asking is not just a statement hiding in the form of a question.

2. He suggests a timeframe for how long the recipient ought to spend on the question (which

helps frame his expectations) and provides a deadline for the response.

3. If he feels the tone might be misinterpreted, he has the human resources department or someone he trusts (like his wife, Jackie) vet it first.

Have you chosen the right medium for the question you want to ask? Have you built in safeguards to ensure that your message is clearly communicated?

Motivate to Action #9:

How can innuendo help me avoid confrontations?

176

If you confront your coworkers about every issue head on, they will come to dread your approach. While plain-spoken language is certainly preferable to lies and platitudes, it can wear thin. If you want to avoid unnecessary confrontation, try innuendo. Innuendo allows you to navigate relationships with a safety buffer, according to Steven Pinker, Johnstone Family Professor of Psychology at Harvard University.

A senior vice president at The Associates, one of the oldest financing companies in the country (they provided the financing for the Model T), wore a pink shirt to work one day, violating the dress code. His boss simply asked, "Everything okay, Bob?" The question presented no risk to Bob if he responded to the explicit question. Bob's boss, however, was giving him an opportunity to answer another, implicit question: "Why are you violating the dress code?" If Bob's boss had asked that question outright, the tenor of the conversation would have turned serious and potentially contentious. By using innuendo, he was politely nudging Bob back into compliance and giving Bob an opportunity to raise a dress-code frustration or another problem himself.

Be careful not to cross the line between innuendo and leading questions, however. "Bob, is there something you want to tell me about that shirt?" and "Are you sure you want to hire that particular candle manufacturer?" are questions that funnel the responder toward a particular answer—your answer.

Sexual innuendos aren't ever appropriate. They're more likely to bring a lawsuit than provide a safety buffer! So be careful when you're making oblique references to decisions or behavior. But don't be afraid to add innuendo to your toolkit of question-based leadership. When used properly, in an unthreatening and discreet manner, they can provide a valuable safety buffer from confrontations.

177

Motivate to Action #10:

How can suspending my beliefs inspire my coworkers and resolve conflicts?

Dan Craft, who wrote a training manual for the FBI, told me that people always act in concert with their belief systems. Their belief systems may not be conventional, but even serial killers have an interior logic that dictates their behavior.

To grow as a person and empower your coworkers, you must suspend your beliefs while listening to others. In doing so, you'll open your belief system to new angles and insights, and your questions won't carry a tone of disbelief or judgment. Not surprisingly, if you demonstrate a willingness to understand others' beliefs, they'll be more apt to embrace yours or accept a compromise. On the other hand, if you demand that everyone subscribe to your beliefs, you'll have few true followers.

Jay Chiat, the Apple marketing genius, kept an index card in his pocket that read, "What if they are right?" Because he was so often right, coworkers rarely gave him much of a fight once he made his opinion known. He needed a reminder that he could be wrong on occasion. He challenged his beliefs, even if everyone else bowed to his authority.

Leaders are not the only ones who are overly protective of their beliefs. If you find resistance during conversations with coworkers, invite them to suspend their beliefs for just five minutes. If you ask and they comply, they'll more likely look for and accept the merit in your position.

Just because your beliefs are deeply embedded doesn't mean that they should be held sacrosanct or that there can't be value in a different belief system. Open yourself up to new perspectives. Suspend your own beliefs for just five minutes.

Motivate to Action #11:

How can feelings and identity make consensus difficult?

In *Difficult Conversations* (Penguin, 2000), Douglas Stone, Bruce Patton, and Sheila Heen identify three root causes of conflicts: identity, feelings, and situation. The situation—the pros and cons for each side—is typically all that's voiced by the participants in an argument. But identity and feelings run deeper, and they can make any situation hard, if not impossible, to resolve satisfactorily for all parties.

For 15 years, one faction in my neighborhood has wanted to install water pumps to reduce algae build-up in the pond; the opposing faction held fast, citing the cost of the project. At a neighborhood meeting, I asked, "How is your identity at stake in this issue?" and "What sort of emotional investment do you have in the outcome?" The conflict became much clearer. The people who didn't live on the pond didn't see how the project would add to their property value, so they felt like they were being taken advantage of. Those who lived on the pond felt that reducing the mosquito population and improving the general appearance of the neighborhood was reason enough for the water pumps. They felt like their progressive actions weren't receiving due respect. Once identities and feelings were acknowledged and assuaged, all the neighborhood members voted unanimously in favor of the water pumps.

Difficult conversations can deteriorate relationships, trust, and motivation for all involved. Ask questions to determine how feelings and identity might be muddying the situation, so that you can get unstuck and move closer toward consensus.

Motivate to Action #12:

When should I use "How" and "What" questions?

When Catherine Smith made her most recent job change (from COO/CIO to CEO of three U.S. business lines at ING), she had to adjust her management style. The front-office and finance managers didn't need considerable direction and oversight—unlike the back-office workers she previously led. In fact, this seasoned and self-confident group would have found that approach insulting.

Her back-office experience gave her insight into a lot of ING departments, but she had to learn how ING's competitors operated and the key drivers to ING's success. She asked her new coworkers to help bring her up to speed on these topics. She asked more questions that began with "what" than "how." In the process, she demonstrated regard for her coworkers' knowledge, skills, and processes. Now, she says, they know they can influence the outcome of decisions, which has created more buy-in, improved decisions, and increased team spirit.

"How" questions can imply a concern about methods. "What" questions generally convey a simple desire for information and confidence in the answerer's abilities to obtain that information. Which questions do you use more with your coworkers? If your coworkers are mounting resistance, maybe you're using more "How" questions than you realize or need.

Motivate to Action #13:

How do I get the best out of my best performers?

You have likely heard the expression "You can lead a horse to water, but you can't make him drink." Tom Steitz doesn't fully accept that logic. Here's his take: "Maybe you can't make a horse drink, but you sure can tie him to a post in the desert for a few days and feed him salt and then see what he thinks about drinking."

181

In 1989, Tom inherited the U.S. men's Nordic combined team. For 78 years, this ski team had been satisfied with just participating at the Olympic level. The medals, of course, went to the historically successful countries—the ones with Alps and legacies of winning.

Tom took a perpetually losing culture and turned it into one that expected to win. When he left, U.S. skiers were often standing on top of the podium, not on the team bus. Now Tom is one of the best executive coaches in the country.

Since athletes are so strong minded, Tom knew he couldn't just tell them what to think. He asked his skiers what they imagined was possible. Next, he asked them to describe their best performance. Finally, he asked them what it would take to bridge the distance between what they'd already accomplished and what they imagined was possible. Then he held them to it.

Tom believes that your team members need to love and fear you at the same time. They won't love you if you try to impose *your will* on them. If you try to impose *their own will* on them, it's a different story.

"You only have the ability to ask them tough questions and face them as a mirror that they know is simply a reflection of what they think. You have to get them to want it for themselves," says Tom.

Your coworkers will love you for listening to and helping to achieve their goals. They will fear you for the disappointment that will occur if those goals aren't realized.

When skiers reached their goals, Tom asked them to set new goals for themselves. These achievers helped inspire other team members with a winning attitude— even if they were at the bottom of the team's rankings. The junior team members could exert pressure with their performances on the senior team members. By applying pressure from both directions, Tom found, everyone wanted to drink "the water."

Tom focused, however, on the top performers. After all, if they achieved their goals, they could make the reward for hard work seem worthwhile. They could also make everyone beneath them aim to reach a little higher.

Underachievers, in sports and business, can take up a disproportionate amount of a leader's time, if you allow it. Tom didn't. He dedicated his time to the winners and the culture of winning. You should, too.

Ask each coworker what they imagine is possible. Together, map out a way to achieve that vision. Then hold them to their "workout plan." Tie them to the post.

Motivate to Action #14:

What is the difference between challenging questions and intimidating questions?

Challenging questions open people up to creative thinking. When John F. Kennedy suggested we put a man on the moon, many challenging questions followed. What materials should we use to build a spaceship? How can we get through the earth's atmosphere? How can a spaceship land successfully on the moon? How can astronauts walk safely in zero gravity?

Challenging questions inspire people to action—to bridge the gulf between possibility and reality.

Intimidating questions shut off creative thinking. Why haven't we done this? How could this have happened? Who was responsible for this? These questions will rot an organization from the inside. When people feel judged, they no longer feel empowered. They no longer want to take risks. They no longer consider innovative possibilities for themselves and the organization. Their fear of censure causes them to close up and take a defensive posture.

According to Tim Welsh, managing partner at McKinsey & Co., if you strike fear in your coworkers, they won't share their true thoughts. Instead, they will try to infer what your point is and present it back to you. He says you "have to create an environment around you where people can share with you their thoughts as they arise."

So, how do you create this kind of environment? How do you find the root cause of a problem without passing judgment and instilling fear? Rather than looking to assign blame, make the search about finding a solution, not finding the problem. Awaken the creative thinking in your organization. Ask, "How might we improve in the future?" not, "Who was responsible for this mistake?"

Motivate to Action #15:

Why did the Catholic Church create the devil's advocate?

Versed in law, advocates are better positioned to represent their clients than the clients themselves—even if, and often *because*, their clients are more emotionally invested in the outcome. Advocates are not bound to strive for the right, fairest outcome. Their goal is simple: to win.

Up until 1983, the Catholic Church canonized saints only after a trial-like process. The prosecutor was known as devil's advocate, his challenger, the *advocatus Dei* (God's advocate). Naturally, for people to be even considered for sainthood, they must have done more than their share of good deeds and gathered a bevy of supporters. Who in their right mind would want to try to dig up dirt on people of such character? And yet, to uphold the high standard of sainthood, someone had to seriously challenge each candidate. As a result, the process guaranteed the devil's advocate protection against retaliation—provided, of course, that he proceeded without malicious, slanderous intent.

There's an old adage that goes: "You can't think yourself out of a problem with the same thinking that got you into it." CEOs often assign someone in the executive team to be the devil's advocate for this very reason. They relieve the designated person of the responsibility of representing her own, the leader's, and/or the organization's interests. This protection against retaliation allows the devil's advocate to vigorously challenge a decision or practice. As a result, the decision often gets cloudier—in a good way. More potential consequences are exposed. New and better decisions are the result.

Ben Shapiro, professor emeritus at the Harvard Business School, takes the devil's advocate process a step further. He encourages CEOs to ask two adversaries in a particular dispute to reverse positions. In doing so, entrenched coworkers are more likely not only to understand their adversary's perspective but also to find middle-ground alternatives—in the process of traveling from one perspective to another. "The best leaders are those who don't take ownership of an idea. They are just looking for the best solution," says Shapiro.

Don't get wedded to any one idea. Be sure to assign the role of devil's advocate, or take on the role yourself, to ensure that the tough questions get asked.

Motivate to Action #16:

How do I gain respect by admitting ignorance and seeking to understand?

John Read, CEO of Outward Bound, was previously a federal policy maker and involved with labor relations. He also worked at Cummings, where he started in the corporate offices then became plant manager of the manufacturing division. He says the experience was like parachuting from the top of a huge pyramid down to this little tiny place on the forest floor. When he landed, he knew virtually nothing about plant operations—unlike the brilliant engineers he was now charged to supervise. The plant's head of operations was a guy named Bill Tubor, who had no teeth, but knew every inch of that plant. He would provide helpful answers only if John asked the right questions. Bill had been at the plant for years and knew he would still be there after John left. John had to prove he listened well and could make the right decisions with the information Bill gave him in order to gain Bill's trust. Eventually, he did, and that is when the game of Cat and Mouse ended.

Mike Harper, former chairman and CEO of ConAgra, shared a similar story about when he was promoted to head of research at Pillsbury. On the first day of his new job, he felt the rush of adrenaline and nerves that accompany many other firsts: the first time in the deep end of a pool, the first time behind the wheel of a car, the first time asking someone out on a date, and so on. Like John, Mike quickly realized that all of his reports (in this case, PhDs in nutrition and food production) knew infinitely more than he did about their work. Rather than hide in his office and pretend to be all-knowing like the Wizard of Oz, he did the opposite. He used his inexperience as a way to make connections with his coworkers and gain their trust. He asked questions that revealed his ignorance and affirmed their knowledge and skills.

People trust and respect leaders who admit the gaps in their knowledge and apologize for mistakes. On the other hand, if leaders act more like managers and do not fill the gaps in their knowledge, they are more apt to make mistakes. And the more mistakes they make, the more their apologies wear thin.

187

Motivate to Action #17:

Why is it so hard to hand off the leadership baton?

As a thriving entrepreneur or leader, you build your business with hopes perhaps that one day someone will liberate you from what you've created. Once you've reached a certain level of security and success, you hand the keys over to a person with the right skills, emotional intelligence, and background to run the enterprise.

The new hire performs many of your job responsibilities, maybe even better than you ever could. So why don't you feel released of your leadership duties? In part, it's because these new leaders don't have the same intrinsic motivation that you have, as the business architect. They don't have the same restless need to meet ongoing demands from the stakeholders. After all, they don't know how hard it was to create and maintain the business's infrastructure.

Entrepreneurs would likely suffocate under all the strains and stresses, long hours and failures, if not for the dream of a serene, duty-free future. And yet, this is a fairy tale for those that don't cultivate leaders in all ranks of the organization as it develops.

Share the mission, goals, and objectives with everyone in the organization. Share the leadership. Only then will you be able to unburden yourself and genuinely relax as leadership is transferred.

Motivate to Action Summary

"Because I said so" is no longer a satisfactory answer for leaders to give. Your coworkers want and deserve better motivation to succeed. Appeal to their desire to be remembered or set an inspirational example for them to follow like Ben Franklin did. Change the question from "Why should we …?" to "How will we …?" or make them stretch to bridge the gulf between possibility and reality (with a particularly challenging, not intimidating, question). Hold them to the goals they themselves set.

Don't ask questions that might suggest that you're coming to an independent decision if it's your coworker's decision to make. Act as a teacher, not a fellow student, and choose the right medium for your questions. Admit gaps in your knowledge, but work fast to address those gaps, since poor recall and apologies wear thin over time. Be sure to assign or take on the role of devil's advocate, so gaps in decision making are discovered. If you're having trouble reaching consensus, check to see if someone's identity or feelings are preventing progress. Once you have achieved consensus, ask the group to say, "Agree," to help cement the decision and everyone's commitment.

189

AFTERWORD

Organizational life is full of uncertainty. The work, technology, and relationships are all in flux. Asking is the navigational system of these uncertain times. When in doubt, ask. And when not in doubt, ask. Learn to doubt your certainty.

When leaders use more questions than commands, the organization's culture flourishes. Uncertainty is seen as an opportunity, not a threat, so curiosity and creativity take root. Asking also confers respect, builds leaders and team unity simultaneously, leads to serendipitous connections and cognitive diversity, and distributes the work along proper lines. So in your office, in the boardroom, in the conference room, at the water cooler, with vendors and customers, at lunch with coworkers or your boss, just ask. Suspend your beliefs for a few minutes, so that real change, learning, and connection are not only possible, but a regular occurrence.

It sounds simple enough, but as I hope this book has shown, not every question is created equal. Just Ask leadership is a mindset, and it needs to be supported and sustained—not just by monitoring your tone and mannerisms, but by a full understanding of what questions can and cannot do, and under what scenarios they are most effective. Some questions stem from idle curiosity and may be counter-productive to your or the organization's goals, while others can cut like a laser to the heart of the matter, carrying the people and the organization with them.

While this book illustrates the value of question-based leadership, it's not a thorough "how to" manual. You will be a better leader, simply by remembering to ask questions like "Whose decision is it?" and "Do you *think*, or do you *know*?" and refraining from *gotcha* questions or *annoyance factor* questioning. But to embody Just Ask leadership and reap the full benefits, you ought to undergo a thorough 360-degree assessment and receive customized recommendations that take into account your coworkers and organization, as well as your individual strengths and limitations.

Just Ask Program

Since writing the book, I have created a Just Ask assessment, training, and coaching program with the assistance of Brian Ferro (president of Aslan Leadership Solutions, Inc.) and Keith Morical (president and CEO of 4ROI, and former contributor to the Wilson Learning Styles and Covey assessments). The Just Ask program will identify what style of leader you are (Professor, Innovator, Director, or Judge) and help you tailor your approach. Unlike Meyers Briggs and DISC, ours isn't a personality test. Your leadership style is, and ought to be, flexible enough to accommodate different, hard-wired personalities.

The Just Ask program rests on four founding principles:

1. The questioner must trust the responder.
   - What is the point of asking a great question if you don't trust the responder? We provide strategies to improve your ability to trust others (without devastating fallout) and overcome blocks that prohibit a safe and equal exchange of ideas and information.
   - We also help you gauge the trustworthiness of your coworkers using seven components (the Seven C's):
     - Capability
     - Capacity
     - Commitment
     - Connection
     - Commonality
     - Consistency
     - Character
2. For a question to be meaningful, it must come from a place of not knowing.
   - The Socratic Method works well for teachers, but not as well in business. Your coworkers will tire of fishing for the answer if it's always your answer they're seeking. They will sense if your "not-knowing" approach isn't genuine.
   - Your stories and beliefs, no matter how rock-solid they appear, aren't always true. And what you knew to be true may no longer be true, due to new developments. You can't

know it all, and even if you could, it would not help engage others.

- Our assessment will measure the difficulty you are having letting go of this "all-knowing" behavior, and our training and coaching program can help you update your approach.

3. The goal of the question must be known.

- Is the goal idea-generating or outcome-producing, or somewhere in between? We help you map out questions along this line.

- Does the asker's goal take into account the responder's needs, abilities, and expectations? We analyze not only question-formation, but also receptivity.

4. Leaders should embrace cognitive diversity by understanding the particular strengths and limitations of their leadership style.

- You likely use the same questions over and over again. We will expand your toolkit of questions to include ones that match your leadership style.

- It's important to recognize that your leadership style (and the questions that accompany it) may not work for everyone or in every scenario. We will help you shift between the four leadership styles (Professor, Innovator, Director, and Judge), to better meet your, your coworkers', and the organization's needs.

Just Ask Workshops

Self-awareness isn't always enough to effect meaningful and lasting change. Often it takes practice or deep immersion to absorb a new leadership approach, which is why we have developed a two-day participative workshop to support the Just Ask program.

For more information on the Just Ask program and workshops, please visit www.justaskleadership.com

INDEX

ABOUT THE AUTHOR

As president and cofounder of ACI Telecentrics, Inc., Gary Cohen grew the company from two people to 2,200 employees and reached $32 million in sales at the company's peak. ACI grew at an average compounded rate of over 50 percent for almost 13 years and was recognized as one of *Venture Magazine*'s Top 10 Best Performing Businesses and *Business Journal*'s 25 Fastest Growing Small Public Companies. Currently, Gary is partner and cofounder of CO2 Partners, LCC, operating as an executive coach and consultant. His clients run a wide range of organizations—from small entrepreneurial companies to multi-billion-dollar enterprises.

Gary received his B.S. from the University of Minnesota, where he triple-majored in International Business, Intercultural Communications, and International Political Science. Prior to attending Harvard Business School (Owner President Manager Program), he attended Covey Leadership Center and Disney Creative Leadership workshops. He has also been a member of TEC (The Executive Committee), an Ernst & Young Entrepreneur of the Year Award Finalist (*Inc. Magazine*), and a Henry Crown Fellow (Aspen Institute).

Gary has served on numerous boards, including Outward Bound National Advisory Board, All Kinds of Minds, Alzheimer Board of Governors, and American Teleservices Association. He is frequently interviewed on leadership issues by *Wall Street Journal Europe, Wall Street Journal Asia, Financial Daily News, USA Today, Washington Post, Business Week, Wall Street Reporter, Venture Magazine, St. Paul Pioneer Press,* and *Profits Journal*. As one of the 100 foremost speakers in the country, Gary also contributed to *Five Star Speakers & Trainers: The Hottest Business Topics from the World's Greatest Speakers* (FIVE PRESS, 2009).